Horace: A Very Short Introduction

VERY SHORT INTRODUCTIONS are for anyone wanting a stimulating and accessible way into a new subject. They are written by experts, and have been translated into more than 45 different languages.

The series began in 1995, and now covers a wide variety of topics in every discipline. The VSI library currently contains over 700 volumes—a Very Short Introduction to everything from Psychology and Philosophy of Science to American History and Relativity—and continues to grow in every subject area.

Very Short Introductions available now:

Available soon:

For more information visit our website

www.oup.com/vsi/

Llewelyn Morgan

HORACE

A Very Short Introduction

UNIVERSITY PRESS

Great Clarendon Street, Oxford, OX2 6DP,
United Kingdom

Oxford University Press is a department of the University of Oxford.
It furthers the University's objective of excellence in research, scholarship,
and education by publishing worldwide. Oxford is a registered trade mark of
Oxford University Press in the UK and in certain other countries

© Llewelyn Morgan 2023

The moral rights of the author have been asserted

All rights reserved. No part of this publication may be reproduced, stored in
a retrieval system, or transmitted, in any form or by any means, without the
prior permission in writing of Oxford University Press, or as expressly permitted
by law, by licence or under terms agreed with the appropriate reprographics
rights organization. Enquiries concerning reproduction outside the scope of the
above should be sent to the Rights Department, Oxford University Press, at the
address above

You must not circulate this work in any other form
and you must impose this same condition on any acquirer

Published in the United States of America by Oxford University Press
198 Madison Avenue, New York, NY 10016, United States of America

British Library Cataloguing in Publication Data
Data available

Library of Congress Control Number: 2023936513

ISBN 978-0-19-284964-9

Printed and bound by
CPI Group (UK) Ltd, Croydon, CR0 4YY

Links to third party websites are provided by Oxford in good faith and
for information only. Oxford disclaims any responsibility for the materials
contained in any third party website referenced in this work.

To
Douglas Cashin
in gratitude for many, many things, just one of which
was loaning an impressionable 17-year-old
David West's Reading Horace

Contents

Acknowledgements

To Ed Bispham, Maria Czepiel, Luke Davis, Catherine Fletcher, Tom Holland, Ágnes Kelecsényi, Matthew Leigh, Victoria Moul, Bijan Omrani, Emily Pillinger, Lilla Russell-Smith, Andrew Sillett, Chris Stray, Helen Wang and Susan Whitfield I am indebted for assistance of many and varied kinds during the writing of this book.

List of illustrations

Chapter 1
Who was Horace?

In the winter of 1900 the archaeologist and explorer Aurel Stein was surveying at high altitude in Chinese Turkestan (modern Xinjiang). Conditions were challenging, the landscape barren and unpopulated, and it was bitterly cold. But his spirits rose when he came across some 'still warm sunshine and a lively stream' where he could camp, and here he pondered his environment with the aid of his favourite author (235):

> It was pleasant to read in the tiny seventeenth century edition of Horace, which always travels in my saddlebag, of the springs that gave charm for the poet to another mountain region far away in the West. And then the question touched my mind: What is this vast mountain world in human interest compared to the Sabine Hills? It has no past history as far as man is concerned, and what can be its future?—unless destiny has reserved the prospects of another Klondyke for the auriferous rivers of Khotan.

Some years later Stein was setting off on his third expedition to Xinjiang, and again he made sure that he brought along a copy of Horace with him. This time it was a modern Latin/English edition of Horace's *Odes* and *Epodes* from the Loeb Classical Library, and he inscribed it in Latin *In ripis Hydaspis MDCCCCXIII*, 'On the banks of the Hydaspes 1913'. Stein was in Srinagar, Kashmir, which lies on the Jhelum or Vyeth, a river to which Horace, in one of his most popular poems, had referred (under its Greek name) as the *fabulosus Hydaspes*, 'storied Hydaspes' (*Odes* 1.22.7–8). Later Stein added, also in Latin, 'This book was a comfort when suffering from a serious injury in the Chinese Nan-shan mountains'. On the occasion to which he was there referring, Stein had been surveying mountains further east when an excitable horse reared and fell on him.

Aurel Stein's expeditions into central Asia brought to light the forgotten civilizations of the so-called 'Silk Road', the cultures that lay between China, India, Iran, and the Mediterranean. He was Hungarian by birth, of Jewish descent, and he had been educated at Austrian and German universities before making a career—initially academic, later more adventurous—in and beyond British India. When he finds consolation in Horace, whether beside that stream in 1900 or bruised and recuperating in camp in 1914, he exemplifies Europe's perception of this Roman author—not just as a poet, but as a repository of core values, a piece of home (Stein's 17th-century Horace was a family heirloom), an intimate guide to living (or to dying), an expression of human civilization. No poet has contributed as much as Horace to Europe's definition of itself.

A more public illustration of Horace's cultural significance is the philosopher Immanuel Kant's influential 1784 essay 'Answer to the Question: What is Enlightenment?', which opens with the assertion that the motto of Enlightenment is *sapere aude*, 'Dare to be wise', from *Epistles* 1.2.40, one of Horace's literary letters. Kant's argument is that Enlightenment—and he was a central figure in an intellectual movement that has done more than anything to shape the modern world—requires a general determination to think for ourselves, to have the courage to apply our individual faculty of reason independently of such controlling forces as the Church or oppressive government. Horace's *Epistles* typically direct advice at young men with ambitions to rise in Roman society, but in a deeper sense Horace had also come to represent a model of mature, independent, worldly-wise living.

This image of Horace, as we shall see, required quite a selective reading of his poetry. But the key point is that, besides being one of the most celebrated of the ancient writers of Europe and its diaspora in modern times, Horace has exerted a more tangible influence on lives lived than any other pagan writer from antiquity. This book will investigate the sources of Horace's remarkable moral authority, but at the heart of any answer will be his peerless capacity for memorable expression of the ethical imperatives of existence.

Quintus Horatius Flaccus was born on 8 December 65 BCE in a small and unregarded town called Venusia (modern Venosa), on the Appian Way in southern Italy. His father was a freedman, a former slave, a status which, in a culture as rigid and class-conscious as Rome, brought with it significant stigma even for his freeborn son. There have been efforts to play down the humbleness of Horace's origins—perhaps, it has been argued, his father had in fact been a freeborn Venusian, captured in military upheavals earlier in the century and quickly released—but this is hard to square with what Horace himself says about the matter. The truth is that his father had been a slave (we know nothing at all about his mother, but the same is likely to be true of her too), but he had the ambition to refuse to let his talented son be inhibited by this accident of birth.

Once freed, Horace's father is described by his son as living the life of an impoverished smallholder (*Satires* 1.6.71), but he also says that his father worked as a *coactor argentarius*, a profession (associated with auctions) which could be lucrative, especially perhaps in the unsettled conditions that obtained in Italy in Horace senior's lifetime. What is not in doubt is that everything that Horace's father wanted for his son was expensive. Unwilling to see him go to the local secondary school with the 'big boys sprung from big centurions' (*Satires* 1.6.72–3), perhaps Roman veterans forcibly settled on Venusia after previous conflicts, he 'had the courage to take me when a boy to Rome to be taught the skills any knight or senator teaches his offspring' (76–8). This was the very best education that could be had, one that situated Horace squarely within the Roman elite: he recalls one of his teachers, L. Orbilius Pupillus, as *plagosus*, 'the flogger' (*Epistles* 2.1.71), but he was a celebrated teacher of literature, commemorated in antiquity in his home town of Beneventum (Benevento) by a marble statue of him seated with two boxes of book rolls beside him. The archetypal pedagogue, Orbilius also wrote a book complaining about 'the wrongs suffered by teachers from the indifference or the excessive demands of parents' (Suetonius, *De Grammaticis et Rhetoribus* 9).

After Orbilius, Horace went on to enjoy the third stage of a conventional elite education, heading to Athens in Greece to study philosophy in the company of such privileged young men as the son of Cicero the orator. Again, this didn't come cheap: Cicero's son was living on 100,000 sesterces per year, an extremely generous sum that Cicero was confident would allow his son not to lose face with the other elite young men he was studying with (Cicero, *Ad Atticum* 12.32.2; 15.17.1). Had Horace's father made enough money to pay for Orbilius' teaching and maintaining appearances 'in the groves of Academe' (*Epistles* 2.2.45), or had the evident brilliance of the young Horace itself opened doors? All we can say is that it is hard to square the education that Horace enjoyed with his insistence that his father was not a rich man, and there is much that we do not know about Horace's rapid social ascent.

It was perhaps an oblique reflection of Horace's circumstances that Aurel Stein was reading beside the stream in Xinjiang, a famous poem by Horace on the Bandusian spring, often supposed to have been located near a villa owned by Horace in the Sabine hills east of Rome, but which was more likely a feature of the poet's childhood landscape in southern Italy. If so, in its celebration of the spring, the poem seems to encode Horace's gratitude for this critical turning point in his life, when he took his leave of the environs of Venusia and travelled to Rome with his father to enjoy the education that would make him a poet (*Odes* 3.13):

> O spring of Bandusia, brighter than glass,
> you deserve sweet wine and flowers as well,
>> and tomorrow you will receive as offering a kid,
>>> brow bulging with his first
>
> horns, which mark him out for love and war—
> to no avail, since he will dye your icy
>> stream with his red blood,
>>> this child of the frisky flock.
>
> You the fierce hour of the blazing Dog-star
> cannot touch, you give delightful chill
>> to bulls weary of the ploughshare
>>> and to the wandering flocks.
>
> You too will become one of the celebrated springs
> as I tell of the holm-oak that shades the hollow
>> in the rock from where the chattering
>>> waters you provide come tumbling down.

Horace's offer of a goat kid on the cusp of maturity to the spring could be understood as being in thanksgiving for his own experiences at an equivalent human age: the life of the young goat is in repayment, by sacrificial logic, for the poet's post-adolescent success. Horace illustrates what he has achieved by bestowing poetic immortality on this landmark in the distinctly unfashionable part of Italy from which he had hailed. In the last stanza the angular forms of the metre resemble the rocks over which the water flows.

But higher education in Athens brought an interruption to Horace's rise, hitherto charmed. To this Greek city full of idealistic young Romans came Marcus Brutus, ostensibly in town to attend philosophy lectures, but actually on a recruitment drive. It was late 44 BCE, less than a year since Brutus had led the conspiracy to assassinate Julius Caesar on the Ides of March. Conflict was brewing between the champions of Caesar's legacy, Mark Antony, and Caesar's heir, the future Augustus (also known as Caesar at this stage), and Brutus, Cassius, and their supporters, who were determined, as they saw it, to restore the Republic, a government styled according to the ancient ways that Julius Caesar's dictatorship had replaced. Many of the Roman students in Athens answered Brutus' call, Horace and Cicero's son among them, and it was as a *tribunus militum* in Brutus' army, an elite officer rank bringing with it the command of a legion (*Satires* 1.6.48), that Horace fought against his future friend and benefactor Augustus at Philippi in north-west Greece in October 42 BCE. The battle of Philippi was a vast, chaotic, and brutal encounter, perhaps the very darkest moment in the internal conflict that bedevilled the last years of the Roman Republic, and which in the event proved a decisive reversal for the republican cause.

Those of the republican forces that surrendered promptly, and Horace was one of them, were amnestied, and Horace returned to Italy. But his father's land and home—his father himself, we must assume, was no longer alive—were confiscated, probably as part of a necessarily huge project to settle all the demobilized troops of Antony and Augustus after the Philippi campaign. From a short biography of Horace that has survived from antiquity (substantially the work of the great biographer Suetonius around 150 years later) we learn that Horace obtained a position as *scriba quaestorius*, very roughly the Roman equivalent of a senior civil servant, securing his financial future at the cost of some social status: the *scriba* drew a wage, something Roman gentlemen emphatically did not.

Once a member of the guild of scribes, always a member, it seems. In his second book of satires, datable to 30 BCE, Horace is still claiming to be receiving urgent summons to discuss scribal matters (2.6.36–7), but by this stage his circumstances have changed beyond recognition. In 39 or 38 BCE, Horace had obtained an introduction to C. Cilnius Maecenas through two friends and poets, Virgil and Varius. Maecenas was one of Augustus' right-hand men, a brilliant, eccentric, and extremely wealthy man who had set out to surround himself with the greatest literary talents of the day. We shall consider shortly what this implies about the poetry that emerged under his patronage, but suffice it to say that from the moment (nine months later) when Maecenas 'invited me to join his circle of friends' (*Satires* 1.6.61–2) Horace's financial circumstances are secure, if also to us obscure. Virgil, author of the *Aeneid* and the greatest of the Augustan poets, had an estate of 10,000,000 sesterces at his death in 19 BCE, we learn, and (then as now) one did not earn much if any money from direct sales of poetry books.

What made Virgil rich were gifts from Maecenas, Augustus, and other admirers, and we know that Horace benefited in similar ways: his villa in the Sabine country is one example, along with a house in Tibur (Tivoli), another resort within reach of Rome (some are convinced the latter can still be identified, and it is available for holiday rents), but the ancient biography states that Augustus 'enriched Horace with several acts of generosity'. Being a 'friend of Maecenas' could entail a range of experiences, but in Horace's case we can add that he developed the closest relationship with Maecenas of any of the poets in his circle. In his will Maecenas requested that Augustus 'be as mindful of Horatius Flaccus as of myself', and surviving poetry by Maecenas addresses Horace in erotic terms (fragment 2 Courtney). On Horace's side, *Odes* 2.17 insists on their inseparability in life or death. A deep affection thus underlies the regular addresses to Maecenas that we encounter in Horace's poetry.

Subsequent political developments offer a broad framework for Horace's poetic career. Between Philippi in 42 BCE and Augustus' final victory at Actium in 31 BCE the two Caesarian commanders, Antony and Augustus, had become irreconcilable enemies, and while two books of *Satires* during the second half of the 30s BCE seem to emphasize the relative calm of much of that period, in the *Epodes* of 30 BCE Horace conjures up the feverish atmosphere of Rome as it approaches the decisive engagement. The three books of *Odes* in 23 BCE reflect the more settled conditions after Actium, with the first book of *Epistles* following shortly after, in 20/19 BCE.

The year 17 BCE marked a climax of sorts in Horace's career when he was asked by Augustus to compose the hymn to be performed at the Secular Games, the emperor's extravagant celebration of the new era of peace for which he claimed credit (Figure 1). A fourth book of *Odes* followed somewhere between 14 and 8 BCE, two further and longer *Epistles* (one addressed to Augustus himself), and the *Ars Poetica*, which may be the last thing Horace ever wrote, but may also fall much earlier. We also learn from the biography that at some point Augustus requested Horace's services as *ab epistulis*, his letter secretary, but held no grudge when the

1. 'The song was composed by Q. Horatius Flaccus' on the inscription describing the organization and performance of the Ludi Saeculares in 17 BCE (*CIL* 6.32323 = *ILS* 5050, discovered in Rome in 1890).

poet refused; and we gather from there and from his own poetry a little of Horace's physical appearance and everyday manner, short and plump, susceptible to conjunctivitis, prematurely grey in his mid-40s, irritable but readily placated.

Most of what we know about Horace is information he shares himself, and he gives us more autobiographical material than any other major ancient author. His is a carefully curated self-image, needless to say, tailored to fit specific poems and with a view to constructing an engaging persona. (It is left to the ancient biography to provide unfiltered information like the mirrors that allegedly lined Horace's bedroom walls.) Greco-Roman literature operated with a strong sense of genre, the inherited rules governing particular styles of poetry and their proper employment. One way in which Horace fosters the illusion of self-portraiture is by choosing genres throughout his career that are broadly appropriate to his own age at the time: the combative forms of satire and iambus in his (comparative) youth; the more placid genre of lyric in his middle age; and the poetic letter, with its implication of retirement, after that. It should be added that Horace's habitual style of self-revelation is tactically elusive, irony his characteristic mode, the gaps and indeterminacies in his autobiography another opportunity for readers to find for themselves there a kindred spirit.

Genre is an aspect of ancient literature we shall encounter regularly, and so deserves a little more attention. There was a hierarchy of poetic genres in antiquity, sometimes tied to the metrical forms often associated with them. Thus the highest poetic genre, epic, was written in a metre called the dactylic hexameter or simply the 'heroic metre', and heroes, humans of superior ability, were stereotypically their subject: so, for example, Virgil's epic *Aeneid* told the story of the Trojan hero Aeneas.

As such, then, when Horace writes satire in dactylic hexameters, satire being poetry concerned with human delinquency rather than human excellence, the incongruity between the poetry and its metrical vehicle is intense and significant. Epic was the yardstick against which other genres measured themselves as well, and so when Horace writes lyric poetry, here too he can play on the relative status of this poetry, insisting on its essential triviality compared to the higher form. In *Odes* 1.6, addressed to another close associate of Augustus, Marcus Agrippa, Horace excuses his inability to do Agrippa's military achievements justice, commends Varius as the man for the job, and of his own poetry says (17–20):

> My song is of drinking parties, mine the battles of girls
> fierce with their nails sharpened against young men,
> when I am fancy-free or a little on fire, in either case
> unseriously, as is my way.

Agrippa gains fulsome praise from this poem, but much of the poem's energy also goes into defining its own limited aspirations as lyric. These conventions offer great scope for creative manipulation, and we see that we are evidently dealing with an exceptionally sophisticated poetic culture: poetry alert to and interested in its own poetic character, and a readership sufficiently well informed to understand and enjoy the poetic game.

Another side to genre is the importance it attaches to previous contributions to the tradition. Horace spends a lot of time in his *Satires* negotiating his relationship with Gaius Lucilius, the inventor of verse satire in its classic form, and in the *Epodes* and *Odes* also, in the Greek poets Archilochus and Alcaeus especially, Horace has charismatic predecessors who require respectful acknowledgement even as he reshapes iambic and lyric poetry for a Roman environment. We will hear more of that in the chapters that follow, but we will also encounter the melancholy fact that almost all the literature that formed the rich backdrop to Horace's poetry—and was familiar to his first readers—is now lost. Consequently a lot of optimistic reconstruction goes into our assessment of Horace's dialogue with his literary models, for which I must apologize in advance. The same is true of a global influence on Roman poetry, the Greek poet Callimachus, active in Alexandria, Egypt, in the 3rd century BCE and a regular point of reference in Horace's poetry, whose promotion of an intellectual sophistication in poetry can also generally only be reconstructed from fragments, often (as with Archilochus and Alcaeus) preserved on papyri excavated in Egypt at the turn of the 19th and 20th centuries. What does survive intact from antiquity, Horace's writings for instance, has done so by being manually copied and recopied from Horace's day until the invention of printing. The former process introduced and perpetuated errors in the transmitted text, and much of the work of classical scholars since the Renaissance has been concerned with restoring texts to their original form. In Horace's case a particularly significant contribution was Richard Bentley's 1711 edition of his works, if only because it showed that Bentley's rigorous application, to this poet's work, of logic and the rules of common Latin usage was not always the dependable guide he assumed it was.

If tradition was a major influence on Horace's poetry, patronage was another, though not perhaps in the way we might expect. Horace's proximity to Maecenas and Augustus is clear, and Augustus' regime was a radical one that recognized its need to shape a favourable narrative. But the role of Roman patrons in poets' work was subtle and indirect. Roman elite society functioned according to a system of mutual obligation. A benefit received placed the recipient under an obligation to reciprocate. Horace, the grateful recipient of a sizeable villa in the Sabine country, was ethically bound to return the kindness, and in poetry he had the ideal currency with which to do so. Thus books and individual poems that he addresses to Maecenas are, among other things, expressions of gratitude. It is essential to this mutually beneficial exchange that its fundamentally economic character—Horace is after all securing a livelihood in return for his poetry—should be veiled, and instead styled as social relations between friends. Horace is not a wage-earner any more; he and Maecenas are gentlemen.

Most pertinently when it comes to poetry, the rationale of gift-giving demands autonomy for the gift-giver. A gift only works as a successful gift if it is independently conceived by the giver, although of course it needs to be something that the recipient will want to receive. The result for literature generated in the gift culture of this time is poetry that is undoubtedly designed to be supportive of the Augustan regime while being shaped by the poetic sensibility of the poet. Horace wrote what and how he, and no one else, chose to write, and a glance at what survives of Maecenas' verse or Augustus' prose should make us heartily grateful for that.

Maecenas and Augustus knew the truth of this as well as anyone, and to take just one example, Horace's focus throughout his poetry on the theme of friendship, *amicitia*, the bonds between Romans who had been cruelly divided by political conflict, was of direct benefit to the regime. However, the emphasis on *amicitia* is peculiar to this poet, even if there is no doubt that there was some sense of a shared mission among the poets of Maecenas' circle. They had in common, for instance, an ambition to create a classic literature for Rome comparable to the Greek literary canon, and this reflected and supported Augustus' claims to be refounding the city of Rome after the chaos of civil war. Deeper commonalities are of course to be found between poets of such social and professional proximity: the passage from crisis to stability between *Epodes* and *Odes*, which reflects political conditions in the late 30s and 20s BCE, parallels in fascinating ways the argument of Virgil's *Aeneid*, for instance, which was composed in the same time frame.

Horace is a poet who has seemed unusually present to the readers of his works—something that emerges from Aurel Stein's devotion to him, as the friend in a book he could turn to in adversity. This sense of familiarity has, as I have argued, ensured the disproportionately high impact of Horace's work on public discourse since the Renaissance. But the strangeness of Horace's poetry should also be emphasized, its origins in political and cultural conditions thoroughly unfamiliar to us, and often not just unfamiliar but abhorrent. Horace has been described—and, on the basis of passages in the *Satires*, *Epodes*, and *Odes*, with perfect justice—as 'the most brutally sexist of the Augustan poets' (Robin Nisbet). He also lives and writes within, and assumes the natural justice of, a slave-owning society, despite his own background. In the final poem of his first book of *Odes* (1.38), Horace strongly implies his sexual designs on a slave boy; while *Epistles* 1.10, on the advantages of life in the countryside, ends with a description of the place where Horace is sitting, not as he *writes* his letter but as he *dictates* it. A slave amanuensis is implied but gains no more definition in the poetry than the verb *dictabam* allows him.

This may lead readers to ask why we should care about the poetic products of this vicious culture at all.

When I read and enjoy Horace's poetry, what I think I am doing is separating the aesthetic from the ethical as objects of my attention—and something like this temporary reservation of moral judgement seems essential if the vast majority of historical literature is going to remain available to us. In Shakespeare's *Titus Andronicus*, as later in *Othello*, much play is made of a key character's race. In the earlier play, Titus' discovery of the plot hatched by the dastardly 'Moor' Aaron, his villainy consistently associated with his skin colour, is in fact communicated by a note pointedly quoting the first lines of Horace's poem that mentions the Hydaspes/Jhelum: 'The man pure in life and innocent of crime | has no need of the spears or bow of the Moor' (*Odes* 1.22.1–2, with a variant Latin text). But we can be alert to the operations of prejudice and injustice in a work of art while still appreciating its artistic merit. No one, of course, should want to imitate ancient Roman society or politics any more than the racist prejudices alive in the Elizabethan theatre, but in both cases there are things to learn through their literature about these other cultures, and about our own in comparison, and things to learn about literature itself. None of that is really possible unless we allow ourselves to enjoy this poetry from another age, and are willing to discover how to do so.

In general, Horace makes the exercise of engaging with his poetry unusually easy. He himself identifies a talent for charming others as a peculiar strength of his, in poetry and in life. He ends a poem in his fourth book of *Odes*, a book much committed to the assessment of his whole career, by attributing to the Muse Melpomene 'that I breathe and please, if I do please' (4.3.24), the doubt of course ensuring that he does please; while in the last poem of his first book of *Epistles*, after contrasting his abilities with his low birth, he describes how he 'was pleasing to the leading men of Rome in war and peace' (1.20.23). His resilience through all the remarkable vagaries of his career bears him out, as does the perception we have of this poet as offering a warm, humane voice even in more recent times.

A special devotion to the god Mercury that Horace periodically voices implies something similar, but in an authentically Roman key. He credits the god with rescuing him from Philippi (*Odes* 2.7.13–14); with the gift of his Sabine villa (*Satires* 2.6.5–15); even with his powers of seduction (*Odes* 1.30). Mercury was Horace's *custos maximus*, 'greatest protector' (*Satires* 2.6.15). In *Odes* 2.17, a poem more contested in its interpretation than most, the close bond between Horace and Maecenas is traced to the compatibility of their horoscopes, and Mercury's special oversight of Horace's life seems to be explained by the disposition of the heavens at his birth. Eerily, using his astrological lore, Horace predicts that he and Maecenas will die at the same time, 'comrades prepared to take the final journey together', and fifteen years later they more or less did. Horace died, just two months after Maecenas, on 27 November 8 BCE, at the age of 56, having left everything to Augustus in a verbal will because the onset of his final illness was so sudden it had left him unable to sign the document. He was buried beside Maecenas on the Esquiline hill in Rome.

Mercury (the Greek Hermes) is one of the most interesting of the pagan deities, a god of interaction, the crossing of boundaries, speech and social grace, himself a figure of eloquence and ingenuity. No wonder Horace, master of wit, irony, and misdirection, understood the trickster god to be his special patron; and readers like Alexander Pope have consistently failed to resist his appeal: 'Horace still charms with graceful negligence | And without method talks us into sense, | Will like a friend, familiarly convey | The truest notions in the easiest way' (*An Essay on Criticism* 653–6). This *Very Short Introduction* is about a remarkably influential poet—one who has managed to persuade people for 2,000 years to read him, but also warm to him.

Chapter 2
Satires

The first that Rome knew of Horace's poetry, or at least what has survived to our times, is a book of ten satires, originally entitled *Sermones*, which appeared in about 35 BCE; a second book followed in 30 BCE. Satire, which to our modern understanding is a mode of expression that extends across novels, stand-up comedy, journalism, and more, was in Rome a tightly defined literary genre, with its dominant strain being that of a poetic tradition begun a hundred years before by Gaius Lucilius and continued after Horace by Persius and, most famously, Juvenal.

What Roman *satura* does have in common with modern satire is a concern with the less edifying aspects of human existence, our vices and physical, animalian impulses—eating and excreting taking precedence over anything more refined. It was a poetry of, often aggressive, criticism; and as such, we might expect the seventh poem of Horace's first book, recounting an acrimonious court case in a city in Asia Minor, to be typical of his satire (1.7.1–6):

> How the pus and poison of Rupilius Rex the outlaw
> suffered the vengeance of the cross-breed Persius, I suppose,
> is well-known to all the barbers and customers of eye-ointment.
> This Persius was a wealthy man with vast business interests
> at Clazomenae, and also an ill-tempered lawsuit with Rex,
> a tough customer, potentially even nastier than Rex was.

It is 42 BCE, in the tense run-up to the battle of Philippi. The litigants in the case are Rupilius Rex, whose second name means 'King', and Persius, a half-Greek local businessman, and Horace doesn't like either of them. The case is presided over by Marcus Brutus, who had led the conspiracy to kill Julius Caesar on the grounds that Caesar was pursuing regal power in defiance of Roman tradition. As Rex and Persius battle it out, they conform to ancient ethnic stereotypes: Persius, the half-Greek, praises Brutus in exaggerated, sycophantic terms, while Rex sets about Persius in rough and ready fashion like an Italian peasant.

The poem ends with Persius' exasperated appeal to Brutus to do what he's good at: assassinating 'kings' (32–5):

> But Persius the Greek, after this dousing with Italian vinegar,
> cries out, 'In the name of the great gods, Brutus, I implore
> you: you're in the habit of killing kings, so why don't
> you slit this King's throat? It's right up your street, believe me!'

This is satire as we recognize it, aggressive and crude. Horace likens what he writes to barbershop gossip, and the protagonists are presented to us in the most unflattering terms, 'pus and poison'; the sneering 'cross-breed'. It is also current material, and controversial: the violent death of Caesar, Augustus' father by adoption, was still a sensitive topic. In fact this poem, with its invective and political urgency, will prove in certain respects to be quite *unrepresentative* of Horace's satirical output, but let's first consider what it does have in common with the rest of the collection.

The circumstances and protagonists are squalid, and the style of expression matches them, low and colloquial. The title Horace himself gave his satirical collections, *Sermones*, means 'conversations', and the idea that the author is addressing us informally, perhaps at dinner, explains much of the character of this poetry. What sharpens the effect is the metrical form of

Horace's satire, the dactylic hexameter, which was the signature metre of the very highest Greco-Roman literary form, epic poetry. Those last four lines of 1.7, without ever being unmetrical, flout all the unwritten rules of respectable poetry, the verses broken up between sense units, the line cadence disrupted, ugly collisions of vowels. The last words especially will have been pronounced *operuwocc, mihi crēde, tuōruwst*, an undifferentiated smudge of vowel combinations, are gloriously incongruous, prose in verse.

Similarly 'conversational' are the organizational principles of Horace's satires, or rather the lack of them. The end of 1.7 is stylistically in the basement, as noted, but Persius' weak and desperate pun would be an underwhelming conclusion to any poem. Elsewhere Horace asserts *ad Regem redeo*, 'I return now to Rex', then does no such thing. Poem 1.7 has not been universally appreciated by scholars, it's fair to say, and a common criticism of this satire and others is the difficulty in discerning a coherent argument within them. Horace seems even to endorse such scholarly strictures by denying satire's claim to be poetry at all. In his fourth satire he excludes himself 'from those I'd recognize as poets' and contrasts satirical verse with an excerpt from the *Annals* of Ennius, the national epic of Rome before Virgil's *Aeneid* displaced it. Write out Ennius' words 'When grim Discord | broke ope the iron-clad posts and gates of War' as prose, Horace says, and you'd still find *etiam disiecti membra poetae*, 'the limbs of a poet, albeit dismembered' (*Satires* 1.4.39–62). Write out 'It's right up your street, believe me!' as prose, in contrast, and prose it stays. But it takes skill to appear so slapdash, to write verse that can pass as prose, and not for a second is Horace's assessment of his own poetry to be taken at face value. There will be more than enough evidence in this book of Horace's meticulous habits of composition, and the very same poetic sensibility is at work in his satire.

What unites these observations about 1.7, and also clarifies Horace's decision to write in this of all poetic genres, is the figure of Gaius Lucilius, whose thirty books of satire written at the end of the 2nd century BCE now occupy less than a single volume of fragments. Lucilius had established the fundamental character of satire for his successors, its conversational style, lowbrow subject matter, and the heroic hexameter as its preferred, though paradoxical, vehicle. Horace's relationship with this model is a regular issue, implicitly and explicitly, in the first book of *Satires* especially. In 1.7, he directly imitates a satire of Lucilius which had (in similar fashion) described a trial contested between two equally obnoxious parties, Quintus Mucius Scaevola and Titus Albucius. Albucius, like Horace's Persius, displayed objectionably Greek tendencies, reflected again in his flamboyant style of speaking, and the poem had ended, again like Horace's imitation, with a weak joke delivered by one of the protagonists. But Horace's reasons for modelling his poem on Lucilius' from nearly a century earlier need a little further consideration.

One reason was that this is just what Roman poets habitually did, setting any new contribution to a genre in the context of its longer history. (Horace's alertness to the rules of genre is just one thing that exposes his claim not to be writing proper poetry at all.) But Lucilius was not just any run-of-the-mill satiric predecessor. By Horace's day he had become nothing less than a Roman cultural icon, his often aggressive style of satire being felt to embody the value of *libertas* (freedom and free speech)—and this made Lucilius' poetry an expression of Romanness itself, since *libertas*, so the Romans fondly believed, was the characteristic condition of the Roman citizen. Some years later Seneca could signal the restoration of *libertas* in Rome with the accession of the Emperor Nero in 54 CE by the simple recourse of modelling his satire on the death of Nero's predecessor Claudius, the *Apocolocyntosis* ('Pumpkinification'), on a poem by Lucilius. Lucilius embodied Rome in its proper state, we might say, and for Horace to write poetry in the 30s BCE that places itself firmly in the tradition of Lucilius is to claim himself, his patron Maecenas, and Augustus' regime as champions of that precious Roman *libertas*. The politics of this poetry are subtle but audacious, in circumstances where Augustus' rivals to power could be characterized as threats to the continued existence of Rome itself, and Augustus himself was a revolutionary masquerading as a traditionalist.

But I have already indicated that 1.7 is in some respects distinctly unlike the rest of Horace's satire. Juvenal depicts Lucilius as 'raging as if with sword drawn' (1.165) against his political enemies, and in 1.7 Horace is clearly channelling Lucilius' celebrated *libertas*, violently attacking his targets (and it's noteworthy that they are in the ambit of his former commander, Brutus). In general, however, Horace's *Sermones* offer a much milder kind of satire. In the first poem of his second book, which is explicitly concerned with his relationship to Lucilius, Horace states that 'this pen will not attack without reason | any living being, and will protect me like a sword | sheathed in its scabbard' (2.1.39–41). That is a fair summary of Horace's style, a sword undrawn in contrast to Lucilius' brandished weapon, notable for its irony and humour, not for invective. The later satirist Persius contrasts how Lucilius 'sliced up the city | —you Lupus, you Mucius—and broke a molar on them' (Mucius is one of Lucilius' victims from his trial satire) while Horace 'slyly touches on every vice of his laughing friend | and once let in, plays around his heart' (1.114–17). Horace's own formulation *ridentem dicere uerum*, 'to speak the truth with a laugh' (1.24), has been felt to capture his satirical approach, with ethics contemplated amicably, laughter and nothing worse the response it evokes from the reader. 'Humour is often more forceful | than abuse, and better at deciding the important issues', he says elsewhere (1.10.14–15).

Some of this missing aggression is deferred to another text, the *Epodes* (discussed in Chapter 3), which, as the dénouement of the Civil Wars at Actium approaches, recovers some of that Lucilian bite and urgency. Circumstances in 35 BCE were rather different, the recent defeat of Sextus Pompey, another rival for power, having ushered in a period of peace. The unexpectedly eirenic quality of Horace's satire is thus perhaps aiming to corroborate renewed hopes of an end to war. As for 1.7, its role seems to be to parcel up and isolate that Lucilian pugnaciousness in a time before Philippi, as if invective is a phenomenon of more chaotic circumstances that is no longer called for.

But whatever the implied rationale of this less confrontational style, the near synonymity of satire and *libertas* in the Roman mind ensures that Horace's collections speak of altered times. 'Libertas' was the watchword of the republican opponents of Augustus at Philippi (Dio Cassius 47.43.1), and one of the assassins of Caesar, Gaius Trebonius, wrote a vicious satire attacking Mark Antony, leader of the Caesarian faction, justifying it on the principle that he and his fellow plotters had as much right to *libertas*, again meaning both personal freedom and frank self-expression, as Lucilius had had (Cicero, *Ad Familiares* 12.16). If freedom of speech seems distinctly hampered in Horace's satires, and authentic Lucilian aggression in abeyance, it is a reflection of the real pressure on Roman cultural expression that an autocratic regime, elements of which patronized Horace, was exerting. Roman satire continued to worry about its relation to Roman *libertas*, and to Lucilius' legacy, for the remainder of its extended history.

Horace's less combative approach can be illustrated by the poem that follows 1.7, a very different kind of satire. (The diversity of Horace's subject matter is another aspect of its satirical disorderliness.) This poem is voiced by a wooden carving of the god Priapus, a kind of divine scarecrow distinguished by an erect and threatening phallus. Figures of Priapus protected gardens and orchards, and in this case the god presides over pleasant gardens on the Esquiline hill in Rome that had replaced a paupers' burial ground, a project of urban renewal overseen by Maecenas. Priapus explains that at night in the gardens their less salubrious past reasserts itself, and describes how on one occasion he witnessed two witches, Canidia and Sagana, conjuring up the spirits of the dead with ghastly rituals in order to bring a reluctant lover to heel. But the witches flee in panic when Priapus, in his terror at what he's seeing, breaks wind with a report as loud as a burst balloon. If you'd seen it, Priapus tells the reader, you'd have laughed out loud. Canidia also features in the *Epodes*, and there she cuts a much more daunting figure, the malign anti-Muse of the collection. Here in the satires, the anticipated reaction of the reader (laughter) and the condition of the cityscape (cleansed and rational), notwithstanding the occasional rough-hewn statue with satyriasis and a cracked behind, point up the very different atmosphere of *Satires* and *Epodes*, the latter (as we shall see) a record of the city in crisis.

Horace's other direct imitations of Lucilius, *Satires* 1.5 and 1.9, seem to select quieter episodes from their model to copy. In 1.5 there is no crisis even when there is a serious political crisis. The poem describes a journey undertaken by Horace with companions including Virgil and Maecenas to Brundisium (Brindisi) on the south-eastern coast of Italy. (Lucilius had recounted a journey he had taken to southern Italy and Sicily.) Maecenas and another figure in the group of travellers, Cocceius, are described as 'envoys despatched on a mission of great importance, | well accustomed to reconcile estranged friends' (28–9), a hint of the purpose of the journey: a summit, possibly in 37 BCE, to restore the frayed relations between the two greatest powers in the Roman Empire, Mark Antony in the eastern Mediterranean and Augustus in Italy. But that is as far as high politics intrude in this poem, as Horace recounts the humdrum inconveniences of travel: the shouts of bargees on the Pomptine Marshes; the gnats, frogs, and drunken humans that prevent him sleeping; a fire in the hostelry; a wet dream he has: bodies, smells, and discordant noises. Scenes are vividly evoked—'the walls of Bari, with its fish' (97), 'Appius's Market, stuffed with sailors and crooked innkeepers' (3–4)—and their vividness seems to guarantee the factuality of Horace's account. Lucilius 'dared to strip off the skin in which everyone walked sleekly | in public, while inwardly foul', as Horace writes elsewhere

(*Satires* 2.1.63–5), and that impulse to expose the truth and dispense with pleasing fictions, in 'real' literature especially, is of the essence of satire. But a further hint of the artificiality of this evocation of the unembellished actuality of things is that Lucilius may also have described a wet dream he had experienced on his travels.

If Roman satire had a natural habitat, it was the *cena* or dinner by invitation, a central cultural institution of the Roman elite. The *cena*, in principle at least, was a space where Roman males came together to socialize and speak freely, a venue for citizen *libertas* in other words, the unfettered self-expression that was a Roman's birthright. The *cena* was also 'the most effective promoter of friendship' (Plutarch, *Cato the Elder* 25.3), and *amicitia*, the ties that bound Romans together (but had failed so manifestly in recent times), occupied Horace in all his writings. Friendship is an underlying theme in 1.5 too, uniting the travellers on their journey to reconcile rivalrous warlords. In *Satires* 2.1, Horace compares Lucilius' books, and thus his readers, to friends (2.1.30–4): 'Long ago Lucilius would entrust his secrets to his books | as if to trusted friends, turning nowhere else but his writing whether | it had turned out well or badly. The result is that the whole | life of the old man is open to see as if painted on a votive | panel'. Horace's main point here is to claim an autobiographical character for Lucilius' satire, and for his own—and it's true that we learn, or seem to (neither satirist's poems were quite the exercise in unvarnished self-revelation that Horace suggests), more about Horace from his satires than from any other of his works.

One such glimpse into Horace's day-to-day life is offered in 1.9, where Horace describes how a casual stroll through the Roman Forum (Figure 2) was interrupted by a man fishing for an introduction to Maecenas and resisting all Horace's efforts to brush him off. The rapid-fire exchange between pushy stranger and a polite but increasingly desperate poet is vividly recreated (1–11):

2. The Via Sacra, 'Sacred Way', through the Roman forum, down which Horace was strolling when accosted by his pest.

I happened to be walking down the Sacred Way, as is my habit,
pondering some trifle or other, entirely lost in it.
A man known only to me by name runs up
and seizing my hand says 'How are you, my dear chap?'
'Fine, right at this moment', I say, 'And all the best to you.'
When he pursued me, I get in first: 'Nothing else, is there?' But he
replies, 'You should get to know me. I'm an intellectual.' At this,
'I respect you for it', I said. Desperately trying to get away,
I now walked faster, sometimes stopped, whispered
something or other to my slave, while sweat flowed
down to my ankles.

Friendship is an issue here, too, the enlightened nature of the
relationship between Horace and Maecenas emerging from the
other man's mercenary misconception of it, and again this works
to associate the regime with a revival of traditional Roman values.
One way of understanding the trajectory of Horace's first book of

Satires as a whole is as an episodic account of Horace's entry into this charmed circle. In 1.6, which provided much of my biographical material in the first chapter, we learn of Maecenas' liberal idea of human worth, illustrated by Horace's own humble origins (and the formative influence of his freedman father), and discover how the poet had entered Maecenas' friendship.

When Horace discusses Lucilius in the first book he acknowledges the latter's role in shaping the satirical genre, but is also openly critical of his predecessor, and this again is typical of an ancient poet creating the space for his own contribution to a literary tradition. Lucilius' greatest failing, according to Horace, was that (1.4.9–10) 'he would often in an hour, | as if it was impressive, dictate two hundred lines standing on one leg', that is, without any effort. The fundamental problem, Horace insists, is that Lucilius' verse lacked refinement (1.10.67–71):

> but if
> fate had postponed his appearance until this age of ours,
> he would be filing away a lot from his work, cutting back
>   everything that
> dragged on beyond the ideal length, and in writing his verse
> often scratching his head and gnawing his nails to the quick.

The contrasting virtues of Horace's short, polished, and sophisticated satire implied by this are illustrated by the lengths of his poems. We are hampered here by the state of Lucilius' surviving text, but one thing we can say with confidence is that Horace has radically shortened the former's model. Each of Lucilius' trial and journey poems, apparently, filled one ancient book roll, while Horace's first book of satires contains ten separate poems. Horace ironically claims, in its final line, that 1.5 is a long text about a long journey (1.5.104), and Horace's trial, arguably his most Lucilian poem, is just thirty-five lines long. His claim that Lucilius' work lacked literary finesse is an allusion to the aesthetic principles of Callimachus, the Greek scholar-poet of

Alexandria, which exerted great authority among Horace's contemporaries. As Horace was writing his first book of *Satires*, Virgil was composing an exquisite collection of pastoral poems, the *Eclogues*, which were modelled on the Greek pastoral poet Theocritus, and deeply influenced also by Callimachus. The result is a refined, highly intellectual, and allusive style of poetry which evokes the idealized existence of carefree shepherds, though in the process lamenting the sufferings of civil-war-torn Italy.

A Callimachean pastoral idyll is one thing, however, and Callimachean satire quite another. Horace's claim to be writing refined satire is a cleverer and more ironic move than is generally appreciated. How, after all, does one 'refine' the distasteful human behaviour that is satire's bread and butter? The truth is that Horace has compounded Lucilius' crime of inserting his bodily functions into heroic verse by setting *his* bodily functions and sundry sordid experiences in a more elegant version of the same. Satire by either author is an intrinsically contradictory thing, subliterary literature, the application of poetic technique to matter intrinsically unworthy of such treatment. Horace's line on Appius' Market in 1.5, satirically 'stuffed with sailors and crooked innkeepers', uses a sophisticated word order to capture the seedy character of the town, while the speed of his metre as he stops and starts in his efforts to shake off his irritating companion in 1.9 is delicately varied.

At the heart of satire, in other words, is an excellent literary joke, and the paradox of sophisticated satire is brought home brilliantly at the end of the first book. Like Virgil's *Eclogues* this book contains a tidy ten poems, as a Callimachean book should, and 1.10, beside critiquing Lucilius' lack of sophistication, places Horace among the fellow literary artists of his day, Virgil and others, from whom he expects approval for his work (though there is a suggestion that he's writing satire because it's the only genre left). But the last line of this tenth poem punctures any literary aspirations he may have implied. 'Off with you, boy, and quickly

add this to the end of my book' (92). Lucilius has just been
castigated for 'writing two hundred lines before dinner, and the
same number afterwards' (60–1), but that is exactly the image we
are left with of Horace, as if the culminating tenth poem is just a
casual afterthought. It is a choice example of Horatian irony.

Amid all this complex and amusing literary self-definition, we
should not lose sight of the overt concern of satire: human vice
and its correction. Horace's satire may eschew invective, but it
offers nonetheless a broad and generous kind of moral instruction,
albeit and inevitably not always to modern taste. The first three
poems of book 1 establish the tone of the collection before the poet
comes into greater focus in the centre of the book. They tackle
various ethical issues such as discontent with one's lot, unhealthy
attitudes to money, sexual incontinence (the sexually explicit
passages in 1.2 have been prime candidates for bowdlerization),
and tolerance, and the poems display the conversational lack of
structure with which we are already familiar. In the first poem, for
instance, an initial statement of the universal human tendency to
believe that the grass is greener over the fence shifts into a critique
of an attachment to money for its own sake, with the two strands
awkwardly combined in the conclusion. So loose is the style of
argument that some have thought we are being encouraged to
doubt the value of the guidance or the competence of our moral
guide, but this underplays the power of the conversational style,
and the congenial, unthreatening personality that is projected. In
a later reference back to these poems Horace talks of 'Bionean
sermones and black wit', associating his moralizing with the
popular homilies (*sermo* can come close in meaning to 'sermon') of
Bion of Borysthenes, an itinerant philosopher in the 4th and 3rd
centuries BCE. Horace and Bion share the aim of delivering
philosophical insight in a homely, accessible style. A further
consequence is that, while Horace's satire is philosophically
informed (and the Epicurean ideal of retirement to a placid life is
prominent), it is also determinedly undoctrinaire, with only
dogmatic and unrealistic principles rejected: at the end of 1.3,

Stoic claims about the *sapiens* or wise man, the perfectly virtuous ideal, in practice unattainable, are held up for ridicule, as indeed they had once been by Lucilius.

We have glimpsed already the first poem of the second book of *Satires*, a dialogue between Horace and C. Trebatius Testa, a distinguished legal authority, in which the legalities of continuing to write satire are playfully canvassed. The poem includes the most explicitly positive reference to 'Caesar', the future Augustus, and in the process associates Caesar and Maecenas with Lucilius' friends Gaius Laelius and Scipio Aemilianus, who could be considered the leading lights of a golden age of Roman political culture back in the 2nd century BCE. But to us, at least, the equation of Augustus with a republican figure like Aemilianus is as unpersuasive—the situations as fundamentally unalike, much as Augustus might have liked to suggest otherwise—as Horace's aspirations to the *libertas* of Lucilius. More locally, with its dialogue format (after mainly monologues in the first book), 2.1 heralds a 'decentring' of the personality of the satirist. Book 1 is to a large degree all about Horace, or at least the persona Horace projected, his views, experiences, personal frailties—and his achievement of personal security. In book 2, with Horace's image now established, the megaphone is handed to a motley collection of other characters, a renewal of Horace's satiric project that eventually turns into a kind of farewell to the form.

Certain satirical preoccupations achieve sharper focus in book 2. The fifth poem skewers the contemporary phenomenon of legacy hunting, the cultivation of older, wealthy people in the hopes of being rewarded with a generous mention in their wills, but it does so in a favourite mode for satire, epic parody. Sharing as it did the metre of epic, while harbouring a fierce antagonism towards the higher form, misuse of epic material and diction came naturally to satire. In 2.5, Homer's encounter between Odysseus and the dead seer Tiresias in the Underworld of the *Odyssey* is reimagined in contemporary terms, Tiresias offering the hero cynical advice on how to restore his fortunes in Rome. Both the impulse to rid epic of its specious mystique and the determined contemporary focus of the exchange between these two mythical figures are characteristically satirical reflexes.

Food, always a congenial subject for a literary form associated with the *cena* and interested in the physical realities of life, particularly one whose very name is associated with foodstuffs comparably stuffed with a variety of contents (we hear of a sausage called a *satura*, for instance), is prominent in the second book, its use and abuse a reliable index of ethical health. In 2.4, Catius delivers himself of a litany of absurdly refined culinary precepts, presented with the reverence reserved for philosophical truths. The Latin word *sapiens*, Catius reminds us, means both a philosophically wise man and a connoisseur of haute cuisine: 'The *sapiens* will get by any means the wings of a breeding hare', he insists (2.4.44). In contrast, we discover at the end of 2.2 that the source of the rustic wisdom on the value of a simple diet that Horace has been sharing, an old farmer named Ofellus ('Porkchop'), had, like Horace, suffered the confiscation of his land, which had been given to discharged veterans after Philippi. Yet Ofellus' misfortune, Horace insists, affected this 'irregular philosopher, of solid wisdom' (3) not a jot, and the farmer assesses his own circumstances phlegmatically (133–6):

> Now the farm goes under Umbrenus' name, recently it was called
> Ofellus's, it will truly be owned by no one, but passes into the hands
> now of me, now of another. Therefore live courageously
> and meet adversity with stout hearts.

A Roman ideal of the independent small farmer, in whom could be found the values that made Rome great, is here given a contemporary makeover.

Now that Horace has largely abdicated his role as guide in his second book, he allows himself to become the target of the kind of criticism he had administered in the first book, albeit in exaggerated form. Poem 2.3 features a bankrupt called Damasippus, who shares the life-changing Stoic doctrine he has learned that everyone who is not truly wise is mad. It is by far Horace's longest satire, its style unusually loose, and Damasippus is clearly meant to come across as fanatical and unhinged, yet even so his criticisms of Horace can hit home. The poem ends with Horace on the defensive (323–6):

> 'I won't mention your dreadful temper.' 'That's enough now.' 'Your
>   lifestyle
> that exceeds your means.' 'Keep away from me, Damasippus.'
> 'Infatuations with a thousand girls, a thousand boys.'
> 'O greater madman, do please spare a lesser, and stop!'

Both 2.3 and 2.7 advertise their dramatic context as a banquet during the Saturnalia, the December festival associated with *libertas* and role-reversal with which *satura* could also claim a special affinity. (None of the multiple ways of explaining the name 'satire' does it any credit: Priapus in 1.8 activates another association, with satyrs.) In 2.7, Davus, one of Horace's slaves, asks permission to speak, and Horace replies, 'Come, take advantage of | the freedom of December, since the ancestors so wished it. Speak!' (4–5). But Horace is less sanguine when Davus exposes Horace's moral hypocrisy, and argues that Horace's susceptibility to vicious impulse makes his master less free than he is himself.

Poem 2.7 represents an immediate corrective to the poem before, 2.6, one of the most popular of Horace's satires. Here Horace celebrated the villa in the Sabine countryside gifted to him by Maecenas, and the simple self-sufficient lifestyle it had afforded him, illustrating his moral with the famous fable of the town mouse and the country mouse. The poet sketches appealingly a dinner in the country, enriched by conversation, a model of social harmony (65–76):

O nights and banquets of the gods! When I myself and my friends
eat before my own household god, and I feed
the cheeky slaves after making an offering. Just as each is inclined,
the guests drain their unequal cups, released
from crazy rules, whether they take their drinks neat,
hard-headed, or water them down and grow drunk more
      happily. And so
conversation (*sermo*) arises, not about other people's villas or
      town houses,
nor whether Lepos dances well or not, but we discuss what matters
more to us, and not to know is wrong: whether
it is by wealth or virtue that people thrive,
or what leads us to friendships, self-interest or right,
and what is the nature of the good, and what its highest form.

In 2.7, the response to this utopian scene, Davus offers a satire on
Horace's satire, subverting not only Horace's self-image in 2.6 but
also the complacent moral authority of book 1 that 2.6 echoes and
encapsulates: Horace engages in amusing self-exposure, but the
destabilizing of his ethical voice is appropriate to the penultimate
poem in the collection, as his experiment in satire winds down.
A poem as invested in the question of freedom as 2.7 is, being
voiced by a slave at the Saturnalia, also advances an interesting
redefinition of *libertas*, a key concern of satire and of Roman
public life but one, as already noted, under unprecedented
pressure with the rise of autocratic rule. Here it is presented as a
philosophical and ethical rather than political principle (Davus
argues like a Stoic philosopher), something achieved by personal
self-discipline. Horace's successor in satire, Persius, a doctrinaire
Stoic, would pursue that idea in his remarkable fifth poem.

Satires book 2 ends as a book of satires should, untidily. In the
final poem of the book, 2.8, Horace asks Fundanius, an author of
comedies (and thus an appropriate voice for Horace's satire), to
describe to him a disastrous dinner at the house of Nasidienus,

another to set too great store by food. As an eighth poem, it already feels like a premature place to round off a book, but the poem itself then also concludes in an extremely unsatisfactory way, as Fundanius and the other guests stage an abrupt departure from Nasidienus' *cena* to escape the host's endless, pretentious descriptions of the food he has been serving them (2.8.93–5):

> we fled him, taking revenge
> by not tasting a single thing, just as if
> Canidia, worse than African snakes, had breathed on it.

To abandon dinner is symbolically to give up on satire, while the name of Canidia looks forward to the *Epodes*. But perhaps the most interesting thing about Roman satire is that the slipshod character of this conclusion to a poetic collection could be felt as a token of Roman authenticity and integrity.

Chapter 3
Epodes

Horace's book of *Epodes* has certainly counted, over time and as a whole, as his least popular collection. The exceptions are the second of the seventeen poems contained in the book, which evokes an idyllic pastoral lifestyle, up until an abrupt correction at the very end (which allowed for tactical excerption in anthologies and translations), and to a lesser extent *Epodes* 13 and 14, both of which anticipate the character of the *Odes*, the poetry, to be described in the next chapter, that has done most to shape Horace's reputation. (The very title of the *Epodes* makes them sound like an appendage to that more celebrated achievement.) In contrast *Epodes* 8 and 12, graphically misogynistic attacks on an ageing lover, have tended to be censored. This indicates already what a motley gathering of poems the *Epodes* represents. But understanding what such a range of poems might have in common will introduce us to one of the most fascinating traditions in Greco-Roman literature, iambus, and will clarify also why Horace turned to it for a book of poems one aim of which was to convey the atmosphere of crisis, tinged with just a tentative hope, preceding Augustus' conclusive victory in the Civil Wars.

'Iambic' may suggest to us a particular metrical foot, the iamb (short-long, unstressed-stressed, di-dum), familiar from Shakespeare's blank verse and countless other places. 'Iambus' in antiquity denoted that foot, and verse in a range of poetic genres based upon it, but also the style of poetry composed by two early Greek authors in particular, Archilochus (7th century BCE) and Hipponax (6th century BCE). This was 'blame poetry', characterized by aggression, extreme vulgarity, explicit vocabulary, and rampant misogyny. 'One great thing I know', wrote Archilochus: 'to pay back with terrible harm the one who does me harm' (fragment 126). The ancients attributed to the iambic foot itself an innate energy that fuelled this vitriolic impulse.

Both Archilochus and Hipponax had a core 'biography' around which their poetry was structured. In Archilochus' case, the story was that he had been promised the girl Neobule in marriage but her father had broken his oath. In righteous revenge Archilochus attacked Neobule, her younger sister, and their father Lycambes, detailing his sexual activity with both daughters until all three of them hanged themselves out of shame. Hipponax's story was modelled on Archilochus': *his* vendetta was against two artistic brothers called Bupalos and Athenis who had caricatured him, Hipponax being notoriously ugly. Bupalos was also supposedly driven to hang himself.

In *Epodes* 6, Horace acknowledges his debt to these Greek 'iambists', and also illustrates some of the peculiarities of iambus. Here is the whole poem, with the poet mercilessly laying into an unnamed and only vaguely characterized adversary:

> Why do you harry undeserving strangers, a cowering
> dog against wolves?
> Why not turn your empty threats here, if you can,
> and attack me, who will bite you back?
> For like a Molossian hound or a sandy Spartan,
> loyal defenders of shepherds,
> with ears pricked I will pursue through the deep snow
> every fleeing predator.
> But you, when you have filled the wood with fearsome barks
> sniff the food that's thrown to you.

> Beware, beware! Savagely against malefactors
>> I brandish my ready horns,
> like the spurned son-in-law of untrustworthy Lycambes
>> or Bupalos' relentless foe.
> If anyone attack me with malicious tooth,
>> shall I whimper like a child and not seek revenge?

Towards the end of the poem Horace reminds us explicitly of his Greek models Archilochus and Hipponax, but the animal imagery—dogs, wolves, and later, rather abruptly, Horace becomes a bull—in its own way evokes iambus' earthy character: the animal fable was a stock-in-trade for this poetry. An important further observation is the symmetry of the conflict envisioned here: dog fights wolf; or dog bites dog. A feature of iambus is that the unbridled aggression with which the iambic poet assails his opponents makes distinctions between iambist and his malevolent target hard to draw. Here in fact the enemy, attacking strangers, is engaged in the same essential activity as the poet.

A parallel point can be made about the end of this poem. Iambus is bullishly (I choose my metaphor advisedly) masculine. We'll see more evidence of this, but here the horns of a bull and bite of a dog (elsewhere it's the sting of a wasp) parallel a common ancient idea that iambic poetry was a kind of weapon, especially an arrow: the Roman epigrammatist Martial talks of Archilochus' 'shafts dripping with the blood of Lycambes' (7.12.6). But iambic poets were notorious also for betraying their own weakness. The orator Dio Chrysostom, comparing Archilochus with the first and greatest of the Greek poets, Homer, tells us that while Homer praised nearly everything (he generalizes slightly), Archilochus did the opposite, criticizing everything, 'and started with himself' (33.11–12). The image we are left with at the end of Horace's poem, a vulnerable child, is at striking variance with the tone of what precedes it. Iambic revenge seems like a zero-sum game, dog-eat-dog, the violent aggression of the iambist being the only thing that prevents his abject humiliation. The iambic aggressor always has the potential to become the target of aggression, the hapless victim.

The title of Horace's collection, *Epodi* in Latin (most likely the name that Horace himself gave it), helps to clarify the nature of his relationship to this iambic tradition. Epode or *epōdos* denotes the second verse of a couplet, then the couplet itself, and then by extension a poem consisting of such couplets. Archilochus wrote such epodes, and it seems that his epodic poems were placed first in the influential edition of Archilochus' poetry, emerging from the academic culture of Hellenistic Alexandria, that Horace's contemporaries would have consulted. In other words, Horace's dominant model is Archilochus, with Hipponax a secondary presence. Almost all of the verse combinations that Horace uses in the *Epodes* can be traced to Archilochus, and the rest in all likelihood could be if more of the latter's poetry had survived. A word similar to *epōdos*, incidentally, is *epōdē*, meaning a magic spell, and the possible relevance of that will emerge later.

As was the case with Lucilius and satire, the character of Horace's literary model is key in his imitation. This is especially the case when a form is as bound up as iambus is with its charismatic authorial figure. The persona projected by Archilochus is sufficiently conveyed by an ancient description of him as 'a man who displayed his poetic ability in extremely shameful and licentious subject matter and revealed a character that was licentious and impure' (Origen, *Contra Celsum* 3.25). But this rogueish figure nevertheless embodied certain civic values that partly explain Horace's decision to make Archilochus his primary model at this juncture in Roman history and his own life.

Archilochus' uninhibited candour about his own and others' failings could claim for the poet, as in Lucilian satire, the all-important value of *libertas*, freedom or frankness, the defining possession of a Roman citizen, and this contemporary force is as evident here as it is in the *Satires*. In *Epodes* 1 and 9, poems emphatically placed at the start and mid-point of the collection, Horace addresses the civil conflict between Octavian (the future Augustus) and Mark Antony, and specifically the climactic encounter at Actium. The first poem anticipates the sea battle; and while the chronology of 9 is elusive (deliberately so), we seem to be in the midst of the Actium campaign—Augustus' victory is never explicitly achieved in this collection, at any rate. In poem 9, the enemies of Augustus, both Sextus Pompey, earlier in the 30s BCE, and Antony, are tarred with associations to slavery: the negation of Roman citizen *libertas*. Pompey had 'threatened Rome with the shackles that he had removed | from his friends, treacherous slaves' (9.9–10), thus simultaneously consorting with the non-free and plotting Rome's enslavement, each, to a Roman, a shocking repudiation of the critical distinction between the free and unfree, Romans and the Rest of the World. As for Antony, his alliance with the queen of Egypt has led to a situation where 'alas!—our descendants will refuse to believe it! | —the Roman soldier, sold to a woman, | carries stakes and weapon at her command and can bring himself | to be the slave of wrinkled eunuchs' (9.11–14). That Roman soldier reduced to servitude to Cleopatra and her eunuchs, driven even to the unspeakably effeminate recourse of mosquito nets, may be Antony himself or a representative Roman member of his army, but either way this is unconscionable.

Epode 1 illustrates another positive value associated with iambus as with satire: *amicitia* or friendship. The poem builds out of the relationship between Horace and Maecenas an idealized picture of something that, as we have already seen, was felt to be the key ingredient of Roman social cohesion, and something concomitantly absent during the dark years of civil conflict. The opening lines of this poem (1.1–4) convey the strength of Horace's bond with Maecenas, and simultaneously of Maecenas' with Augustus:

> On Liburnian galleys you will go, my friend,
> > amid the high ramparts of ships,
> all prepared to endure every peril of Caesar
> > at your own peril, Maecenas.

The first two lines are worth seeing in Latin: *Ibis Liburnis inter alta nauium, | amice, propugnacula.* A 'Liburnian', the kind of warship that Maecenas will be crewing at Actium, was a small, manoeuvrable craft (Figure 3). There is a contrast with the bigger vessels deployed by the enemy, their size conveyed explicity by *alta*, 'high', and by the huge word *propugnacula*, 'ramparts, bulwarks'. The word denoting Maecenas here, *amice*, 'my friend', is dwarfed by the words for Antony's vast craft that surround it. Friendship, touted here at the outset of this collection, stands as a potential solution to the grim world depicted in the *Epodes*, but it is a vulnerable, imperilled value, and violent enmity a more dominant presence in the collection.

3. Representation of a small, manoeuvrable 'Liber’nian' ship, from the plaster cast of Trajan's Column in the Victoria and Albert Museum.

Relevant here are the various roles adopted by the speaker of the *Epodes*. Two particularly interesting ones derive from the Greek iambic tradition, the iambic poet at times depicting himself haranguing the city in some public role and, at other times, for example in poem 13, addressing a more select group of friends at a *symposium* or drinking party, an important Greek social institution which we'll consider at greater length in Chapter 4—the drinking party is the traditional venue for lyric poetry like Horace's *Odes*. Suffice it to say now that this gathering of friends is another way in which *amicitia* persists in this collection, but again its presence is tentative. A significant moment that we shall revisit in Chapter 4 is when Horace opens *Epode* 9 by asking Maecenas 'when', *quando*, they will be able to celebrate Caesar's victory over Antony and Cleopatra with drinking and music—the *Epodes* position themselves quite carefully *before* the definitive conclusion of the war, a poetry of conflict and crisis to the end.

The public persona introduces another dimension of iambus, a fundamental concern it has for the condition of the city. The iambist can sometimes cast himself in the role of a Jeremiah, berating the citizens for their vices ('O indigent citizens, hear my words!' demands Archilochus in fragment 109). Two remarkable poems within the *Epodes* illustrate this, and both, poems 7 and 16, seem to envisage the very direst future for Rome.

'Where, O where are you blindly rushing in your guilt? Or why are swords | that were sheathed grasped in your hands?' Horace demands of his fellow Romans at the start of *Epode* 7 (1–6):

> Not in order that the Roman might burn
>   the haughty citadel of jealous Carthage,
> nor that the Briton, as yet unmolested, might walk down
>   the Sacred Way in chains,
> but that, in answer to the Parthians' prayers,
>   this city might perish by its very own hand.

Carthage had been Rome's ancient, archetypal foe, now long destroyed; Parthia, a power to the east of the Roman Empire, was its current existential enemy. The passage illustrates the horror that Romans felt when their military prowess was not directed towards bringing Roman civilization to the benighted, but was instead turned against their own fellow Romans in civil war. This seemed a horrible reversal of the natural order—better by far if captives from a conquest of Britain could be herded through the centre of Rome in a triumphal procession.

Horace's question receives no response from a citizenry stupefied, by fear, guilt, or maybe a curse, and he answers it himself (17–20):

> bitter fate harries the Romans
> and the crime of a brother's murder,
> ever since blameless Remus' blood spilled
> on the earth, a curse to his descendants.

In the course of founding the city of Rome, Romulus had killed his own twin brother, and Romans seven centuries later are cursed to repeat this abominable crime, he says. Civil war is a kind of fratricide, and the diagnosis is that this obscene contravention of basic human ties is in Rome's very DNA. The atavistic force of this poem is underlined by Cicero's notion (Cicero, *Tusculan Disputations* 1.1.3) that Archilochus' life in the Greek islands had coincided in time with the reign of Romulus in Rome.

The counsel of *Epode* 16 is comparably desperate (1–10):

> Already a second age is being ground down by civil wars.
> and Rome is falling through its own strength.
> The city that neither neighbouring Marsians had the power to destroy
> nor the Etruscan force of menacing Porsena
> nor Capua, our valiant rivals, nor fierce Spartacus
> nor the Gaul, faithless in time of revolution,

nor wild Germany conquered with its blue-eyed warriors
    nor Hannibal, a figure of ill omen for parents,
we will destroy, an unholy age of accursed ancestry,
    and wild animals will again occupy the ground.

Again it is a genetic disorder afflicting Rome. None of this litany
of historical enemies had been able to destroy the city, not even
Hannibal the Carthaginian, who, nearly two centuries after his
death, Horace hints, was still a bogeyman that Roman mothers
threatened their cabbage-averse children with. In the second line,
Horace plays with a longstanding pun on the name 'Rome', the
Greek version of which, *Rōmē*, also meant 'strength' or 'power'.
That inherent power, self-directed, is bringing Rome to its knees.
In this poem Horace's prescription is a truly shocking one:
Romans' only hope is to abandon their city—to stop being
Romans—and to sail out into the Atlantic to a new home. Truly
the world is upside-down: the most virile of us must flee, Horace
insists (39–40). Virgil, in his fourth *Eclogue* (seen by Christians
as a prophecy of the birth of Christ, and thus known as the
'Messianic Eclogue'), had recently presented a much more
optimistic vision of the future, and Horace's prediction stands out
all the more depressingly against Virgil's hopes of a golden age.

The deep pessimism that pervades this collection, albeit
periodically interspersed with hints of a better outcome, is clear
enough from these two poems, and we shall find it expressed in
other ways elsewhere. Before we investigate Horace's iambic
dystopia further, however, it's worth noting a model other than
Archilochus (or Hipponax) who also exerts a subtle but formative
influence in the *Epodes*. Callimachus, who wrote in Alexandria
(ruled by Cleopatra's ancestors, the Greek Ptolemaic dynasty) in
the 3rd century BCE, exerted the greatest influence over Roman
poets of any Greek literary figure, and his *Iamboi*, an imitation of
Hipponax, represented an important precedent for the *Epodes*. An
illustration will take us back to *Epode* 6, where the rather jarring

shift of imagery from dogs to a bull introduces an allusion to
Callimachus, and a moment in the *Iamboi* where the Greek poet,
like Horace in *Epode* 6, explains and defends his approach to
poetry. It is characteristic of Horace's imitation of some of the
earliest Greek poets, true of his lyric *Odes* too, that it is filtered
through the poetic and scholarly activity of much more
recent times.

Callimachus' influence can be seen also in the peculiar number of
poems that this collection contains, and in aspects of its formal
organization. In both Callimachus' *Iamboi* and the *Epodes* an
initial metrical conformity is superseded by diversity, for instance,
while the number of poems in the *Epodes*, seventeen, is best
explained by assuming that Callimachus' *Iamboi*, thirteen poems
followed (in the texts Horace would have read) by four mysterious
extras, had left it unclear to the Romans where exactly
Callimachus' collection ended. Certainly in *Epode* 14 Horace's
explanation to Maecenas of his failure to finish his book, a
distinctly un-iambic infatuation with a woman, is appropriate for
a poem which isn't sure if it's part of a book of iambics any more.
The poetic play is itself characteristically Callimachean, and a
reminder of the high artifice typical of Roman poetry—which is
nevertheless entirely compatible with a commentary, albeit
oblique, on urgent contemporary concerns.

The diversity of topics within the *Epodes* is typical of iambus: an
ancient critic talks of Archilochus 'sweeping along much that is
disorderly' (Ps.-Longinus, *De Sublimitate* 33.5), an observation
that encompasses the lack of overall coherence in the collection,
the (deliberate) lack of polish in individual poems, and even the
ramshackle character of Archilochus' metres. But that diversity
owes something also to Callimachus, whose *Iamboi* strayed into
accounts of the cult statues of gods, and the origin of a ritual or
a turn of phrase. In important respects, however, Horace has
reverted to the character of early iambus. In his first poem,
Callimachus had introduced his model Hipponax returning from

Hades to announce a softer kind of iambic poetry than he was known for: 'I do not bring the Iambus that sings of the feud with Bupalos' (3–4). Callimachus' *Iamboi* certainly lack the vitriol of their model: one poem celebrates the birth of a friend's daughter. In his *Epistles*, looking back on the *Epodes*, Horace seems to echo Callimachus' formula of an imitation with the sting taken out, stating that he 'followed the metre and spirit of Archilochus, not the subject matter and the words that harried Lycambes' (*Epistles* 1.19.23–4). But the sense is significantly different, as the character of the *Epodes* further indicates. Horace will not engage in a sustained attack on an individual, like Archilochus' on Lycambes, and as with his satire this suppression of personalized criticism is significant, and a reflection of the times—but neither is he adopting the fully defanged style of iambus favoured by Callimachus.

The variety of Horace's *Epodes* certainly extends to their tone. It's hard to take *Epode* 3 very seriously, for instance, a poem in which Horace curses Maecenas for serving him garlic, the effects of which are vastly exaggerated, to the extent of encouraging us to conclude that the poet is offering a playful explanation of the iambic rage that drives his poetic activity. Garlic certainly has, in Horace's account, the tell-tale iambic character of something that both fuels that anger and is the target of it. We have already encountered in *Epode* 6 the peculiarly reciprocal character of iambus, where righteous anger and the wrongdoing that has provoked it merge.

In *Epode* 4 this dynamic is especially striking. Here Horace attacks a social climber, now a member of the equestrian order and in possession of a large estate, who began as a slave. 'As great as the disagreement is between wolves and lambs | by natural lot', Horace insists, 'so is mine with you' (1–2). It is left to the very last words of the poem to reveal that its target was a *tribunus militum* as well. So, of course, had Horace been, and given his own origins under the shadow of slavery (and similar stories attached to

43

Archilochus), from which he also had emerged to achieve the status of *eques*, it is impossible to read this poem without being acutely aware that Horace might as well have been attacking himself. *Epode* 10, which wishes 'smelly Mevius' (as in satire, the impulse is strong to reduce people to smells and body parts) an extremely unhappy sea journey, is similar if, as he does appear to be, Mevius is a poet. Again a figure worthy of expulsion from the community bears more than a passing resemblance to the instigator of the lynch mob.

If such weirdly self-directed conflicts depict a culture in crisis, that is indeed the dominant impression of the *Epodes*. A world in which witchcraft is running rampant is in ancient terms one in thrall to dark forces. Marcus Agrippa, Augustus' lieutenant, undertook a number of policies to improve Rome when he served as aedile (a Roman magistrate concerned with the maintenance of the city) in 33 BCE, restoring public buildings, mending roads, offering free access to the public baths, and clearing the sewers having sailed through them in an inspection until he reached the Tiber. He also expelled sorcerers from Rome (Dio 49.43: astrologers too, who were not universally respected). A figure already familiar from the *Satires*, the witch Canidia, is prominent, even dominant, in the *Epodes*, a suspect in Horace's poisoning by garlic in *Epode* 3 but the focus also of the two longest poems, *Epode* 5 and the concluding poem 17. *Epode* 5 describes a ghastly process in which Canidia, 'her hair and dishevelled head entwined with little snakes' like a Fury, assisted by her fellow witches, seeks to generate a love charm by burying an innocent young boy up to his neck, starving him to death, and harvesting his organs. The boy begs pitifully to be spared, Canidia explains her appalling plan to win back Varus' affections, and then with his dying words the boy curses the witches with an authentically iambic passion. Canidia and her coven will be turned upon by the whole city and pelted with stones (91–102):

> No, even when, bidden to die, I have breathed my last,
> I shall haunt you at night like a Fury,

and as a ghost I shall attack your face with hooked nails,
   such is the power of the Dead,
and squatting on your restless hearts
   I shall steal away your sleep with terror.
The mob, attacking you with stones street by street, on every side,
   will crush you, foul old women.
Then your unburied limbs will be scattered by wolves
   and the birds of the Esquiline hill,
and the sight will not escape my parents,
   who, alas, survive me.

We shall consider Canidia's second major appearance, in the final
poem of the *Epodes*, later in this chapter, but for the moment, let
us say that for all her wickedness, she also partakes of the eery
interchangeability of iambic revenge. The name Canidia suggests
dogs, *canes*, which are notoriously shameless creatures. But in
their characteristic aggression toward outsiders dogs are also
(as we have seen) models for the iambist himself. Canidia also
recalls the bawdy old woman of myth, Baubo or Iambe, to whom
the Greeks traced the origins of iambus, making her the poet's
muse as well as his nemesis.

The poems traditionally suppressed, 8 and 12, introduce us to
another aspect of this form's bleak worldview. In each poem the
authorial figure is intimately involved with a woman who is
presented as physically repulsive and sexually voracious, and
whose appearance is dissected in merciless detail. Here it is good
to remind ourselves how selective a reading it was that extracted
from Horace's poetry a model of civilized decency (8.1–6):

Are you really asking me, you rotten, ancient creature,
   what is unstringing my masculinity,
when your teeth are black and old age
   furrows your forehead with wrinkles,
and a disgusting hole gapes between scrawny
   buttocks, like a constipated cow's?

We get the picture. But it is worth emphasizing just how much such material represents iambus in its element, sharing both unvarnished physicality and the base vocabulary required for it. The woman in question is high-born and educated, one of the elite, Horace intimates, and her physical and sexual shortcomings are thus reflective of Rome's debased condition. Archilochus' private enmities had in a similar way, apparently, been presented as a means to protect the wider community. But in a way that is becoming familiar, we are bound to ask, even as we read the poet's abuse, what it says about him that he is there, in bed, with this woman. *Epode* 12 also shows him failing to perform with a 'woman fit only for black elephants' (12.1), and the same question arises. Equally, the suitability of iambus for describing such old, sexually uninhibited women as Baubo and Iambe is relevant again here.

If the poet is not spared, nor are we. This poetry is designed to provoke disgust in its reader, and an instance of that is perhaps worth exploring by an examination of the Latin. At the end of *Epode* 8, having denied any possibility of getting aroused by his sexual partner, the poet nevertheless suggests that fellating him might do the trick (19–20):

> To stir it up from my haughty groin,
> > you'll have to work at it with your mouth.

If we imagine this poetry spoken out loud (and we do assume that even private readers would have enunciated the words they were reading), the Latin of the last line *ore allaborandum est tibi*, pronounced something like *ōr'allabōranduwst tibi*, makes the reader's mouth do things it might not choose to. In broad terms Horace's poetry enacts a process of progressive refinement from the 'conversations' of satire to the 'songs' of his lyric *Odes* (from food to wine is another way of defining this movement): the *Epodes* sit uneasily between them, with some moments of elevation, but otherwise delving into the very depths.

A characteristic of iambus we have already had cause to note is the coexistence of expressions of exaggerated masculinity and their opposite. The dying, prepubescent boy calling down imprecations on the witches in poem 5 is a salient example. In *Epode* 15 the poet seems to be dismissing an unfaithful lover with manly resolve, but it isn't convincing, and one doubts that Neaera will be especially devastated if he does. In a marvellous turn of phrase, furthermore, Horace ties the weakness very distinctly to his historical self. 'If there is any manhood in Flaccus' (12), she'll rue her waywardness, he says. But while the Latin that I've translated as 'manhood' can carry a similar range of meanings to the English, Horace's *cognomen* (last name) Flaccus literally means 'floppy', 'flaccid'. The note of self-criticism is entirely true to Archilochus, notorious for his willingness not only to excoriate others but to 'say the worst things about himself' (Critias in Aelian, *Varia Historia* 10.13).

An association with scapegoating hangs about iambus, the process whereby an individual, in Greek the *pharmakos*, is loaded with the sins of the community and expelled. Hipponax seems to have marked his enemies Bupalos and Athenis as *pharmakoi*, and the Byzantine poet and scholar Tzetzes cites Hipponax in his account of the ritual (*Chiliades* 5.728–39, 45–6):

> The *pharmakos* was a purification in ancient times of the
> following kind:
> If a disaster caused by divine anger afflicted the city,
> whether famine or disease or some other harm,
> they led the ugliest man of all as if to sacrifice him
> in order to cleanse and cure the city of its disease.
> Setting the sacrificial victim is an appropriate place,
> they put cheese, barley cake and dried figs in his hands,
> whipped him seven times on his penis
> with quills, wild fig branches and other wild plants,
> and finally burned him with wood from wild trees
> and scattered his ashes into the sea and the winds

in order, as I said, to cleanse the city of its disease...
Hipponax describes the whole custom best:
'to purify the city and be struck with fig branches'.

The impulse to identify an enemy common to all, and build a
sense of community on that shared hatred, is in fact hard-wired
into human beings (and thus a feature, not a bug, of contemporary
social media), but two further aspects of scapegoating are worth
underlining. One is that the impulse to isolate and expel a hated
individual is, as Tzetzes emphasizes, the mark of a community
under strain, a sign of crisis. Another is that this process of
defining insider and outsider is inherently unstable, the aggressive
avenger being easily interchangeable with the malignant victim.
In Tzetzes' example the ugliest man became a scapegoat, for
instance, while Hipponax's ugliness was not only notorious, but
the original cause of his feud with Bupalos and Athenis and the
iambic poetry that was thereby generated. Both features are
readily paralleled in the *Epodes*, a collection expressive in general
of the greatest crisis that Rome had ever faced, its own near
self-destruction, and within which texts play disconcertingly with
the resemblances between antagonists. If the *Epodes* hint at a
positive outcome, it is not yet with us, but the allusions to an
extended enactment of the expulsion of a polluting presence from
the city suggest the dark ritual that precedes renewal. What is not
clear is who the *pharmakos* is, who it is that will be driven from
the city to ensure its release from civil war, the witch Canidia or
Q. Horatius Floppy himself.

The crisis affects the poetry. As we have noted, iambic abuse
poetry is sloppy stuff at the best of times (or rather, exquisitely
crafted poetry designed to look sloppy, just like satire). But the
final poem of the collection is a deliberately inconclusive affair,
and leaves the entire collection without the solution it desperately
seems to need. Superficially *Epode* 17 is a palinode, a retraction
by the poet of all his attacks on Canidia: it owes a lot to the most
famous palinode of antiquity, in which the lyric poet Stesichorus,

having lost his sight after criticizing Helen of Troy, regained it by composing another poem in which he insisted she never went to Troy after all. Horace also takes back everything he has said about Canidia—'chaste you are and virtuous, | you will roam through the constellations, a golden star!' (40–1)—and describes what her malign attentions have done to him. The youthful aggression that fuelled his iambic aggression has all gone (21–3):

> My youth has fled, and my blushing complexion.
> I am left just bones covered with sallow skin
> and my hair has turned white with your burnt oils.

But Canidia is having none of it: 'Will you, High Priest of Esquiline sorcery, | have filled the city with my name with impunity?' (58–9) Far from placated, she will pursue him for the remainder of his days.

Horace emerges from this poem damned as a kind of sorcerer himself, his iambic verse interchangeable with Canidia's spells, *epōdos* and *epōdē*. But Canidia's tirade ends on a note of doubt we have seen before in this collection. 'Shall I | bewail the ineffectual results of my magic arts on you?' are her final words (81), and the last of the poem and the book. Will her magic prevail, or will Horace's iambus? The *Epodes* thus end in stalemate, the future poised on a knife edge but inscrutable, whether for Horace or for the city his poetry has sought to cleanse.

Chapter 4
Odes

Nunc est bibendum!

'Now we must drink!' The opening words of *Odes* 1.37, the penultimate poem of Horace's first book of lyric poems, is still a familiar expression, and it will emerge that it amounts to rather more than just an exhortation to get drunk. The *Odes*, four books containing 103 poems, the first three books of which were published as a single collection, are the achievement for which Horace is best known, an astonishingly successful transposition to Rome of a rich and complex Greek tradition. Horace in the *Odes* characteristically says a great deal in a very limited space. These three words can help us in a preliminary way to contextualize Horace's lyric poetry, convey its remarkable ambition, and maybe even begin to explain its lasting appeal.

Odes 1.37 is also known as the 'Cleopatra Ode', as it celebrates the final defeat of the forces of Mark Antony and Cleopatra VII of Egypt by Augustus, at Actium in September 31 BCE, followed by their suicides in Alexandria the following year. In Horace's account Antony is sidelined; Cleopatra, as a female eastern ruler a reliable catalyst for Roman prejudice, is the focus. It is time to drink, Horace declares, because the threat to Italy from the decadent east had been suppressed, and with it the civil conflict between Romans that had festered for twenty years (1.37.1–12):

Now we must drink, now beat
the ground with unfettered feet, now
    it is time to deck the couches of the gods
      with extravagant feasts, my friends.

Before this it was wrong to fetch out the Caecuban
from our grandfathers' cellars, so long as
    the queen was plotting crazed ruin for the Capitol
      and destruction for our rule

along with her debased tribe of men
sunk in perversion, a woman frantically
    pursuing wild hopes and drunk on sweet
      fortune.

The words 'Now we must drink!' also provide a belated answer to
a question that Horace had posed years before, in very different
political and poetical circumstances. '*When* shall I drink with you,
Maecenas, the Caecuban set aside for festal banquets?', Horace
had asked at the beginning of *Epode* 9. There also it was the
(anticipated but still unrealized) defeat of Cleopatra that was at
issue, and the same high-quality (and symbolically, local and
Italian) wine in prospect. But the time to celebrate had not yet
come, was the implication. The dialogue that Horace establishes
between his iambic collection and the *Odes* is partly a function of
the passage of time. The *Epodes* are products of the 30s BCE and
reflect the circumstances of a city at war. By the time the first
three books of *Odes* were published, in 23 BCE, Rome had been at
peace with itself since the capture of Alexandria in 30 BCE. The
Odes remain acutely aware of that traumatic earlier time, and alert
to the danger of returning to it by repeating the moral failures of
the past, but the emphasis is now on the peace that had at length
been achieved.

But the progress from tentative enquiry in the *Epodes* to confident
assertion in the *Odes* is also a matter of poetic genre. Iambic
poetry, as we've seen, is a poetry of crisis. Even when there are

friendships, they are friendships forged by the existence of a common enemy. The 'Cleopatra Ode' is evidence that the same can sometimes be said of lyric poetry, but more typical is an emphasis on the positive grounds for friendship. Even comparing *Odes* 1.37 and *Epode* 9, lyric adopts a less confrontational, more refined style: the aggressive satire in the epode against 'wrinkly eunuchs' and the unmanly use of mosquito nets is now beneath us. To call iambus a poetry of conflict and lyric a poetry of peace, iambus slander and lyric acclamation, is too simplistic, but it does not mischaracterize Horace's approach too egregiously.

In two further respects the opening words of the 'Cleopatra Ode' can help us understand the character of Horace's new literary venture, the first being the Greek model that *nunc est bibendum* was designed to evoke. In the 7th century BCE the poet Alcaeus, from Mytilene on the island of Lesbos in the eastern Aegean, exhorted his friends in similar fashion: 'Now must we get drunk!', *nūn khrē methusthēn* (fr. 332: the *methu-* stem is the same as that in methylated spirits). The motivation for a party in this instance was the death of Myrsilos, a tyrant in Mytilene and longtime foe of Alcaeus and his comrades.

Alcaeus fulfils the same role in the *Odes* as Lucilius and Archilochus in the *Satires* and *Epodes*: he is Horace's primary model. But a further prerequisite of appreciating the nature of Alcaeus' influence takes us back one last time to *Nunc est bibendum*, and specifically to the emphasis on alcoholic consumption. Wine is so ubiquitous a feature of Horace's lyric verse that drinking often functions as a metaphor for this kind of poetry. But the deeper explanation of the prominence of drinking in Horace's lyric is the traditional venue of lyric performance, a Greek institution known as the *symposium*, 'drinking-party', for which the poetry of Alcaeus and other lyric poets was typically composed.

A little time is required at this stage to introduce, first the *symposium*, and then Alcaeus.

The *symposium* was a banquet, but with the emphasis firmly on drinking. It was an elite institution, inherently masculine in ethos, and a participant would typically find himself in the company of established acquaintances. Wine, conversation, and song all promoted the cohesion of the group, and there was emphasis also on equality between participants, freedom of speech, decorous behaviour, and securing the goodwill of the gods towards the gathering. Erotic interest was provided by female musicians or courtesans, and also by boy cup-bearers or waiters: pederasty, the perception of pubescent boys (generally up until the first appearance of body hair) as appropriate objects of sexual interest was a key component of the *symposium*, and Horace reflects this. Thus, as mentioned in the first chapter, in the poem after the 'Cleopatra Ode', the concluding poem of book 1, Horace pictures himself drinking wine and addressing his young waiter (*minister* in Latin), associating himself and his slave with myrtle, the tree of Venus, the love goddess. The poet's intentions are clear enough, and it's a quintessentially lyric scene appropriate to a concluding poem: love-making, like wine, could serve as shorthand for lyric poetry. If pederastic material is rather less prominent in Horace than it seems to have been in Alcaeus' poetry, that reflects an important difference between Greek and Roman sexual mores. Sexual relations between adult and adolescent males, both freeborn, was the height of respectability in Greece, but reprehensible in Rome. Horace's male partners, more visible in the fourth book of the *Odes* than earlier, are by implication slaves or ex-slaves.

As for Alcaeus, to Horace and his readers he was not just a poet but a well-defined historical figure whose poetry detailed an eventful life. An aristocrat, his poetry (little of which now survives;

a familiar story by now) reflected his active role in political conflict in the city of Mytilene, and voiced the cameraderie that existed between himself and his friends and political allies. Such themes were natural to a *symposium* with comrades in attendance, but so also was the rather different material, hymns and love poetry, that also featured in his work. Ancient critics struggled with this apparent inconsistency, dividing his poems into serious *stasiotika* (on political conflict) and trivial *erotika* (love poetry). The ancient critic Quintilian disapprovingly contrasts the poetry 'in which Alcaeus attacks tyrants and contributes much to moral improvement', where his style is 'succinct, grand, precise and very like an orator's', with his less respectable love poetry: 'he was better suited to the higher topics' (*Institutio Oratoria* 10.1.63). But this is all the predictably diverse matter of a sympotic gathering. The variety in topic and register of Horace's lyric has more than one source, but it is licensed in the first place by Alcaeus.

Alcaeus' poem about Myrsilus was an exhortation to his male comrades to celebrate the tyrant's death; Horace's imitation is addressed to his *sodales*, a word denoting 'bosom buddies', on the occasion of the death of (by implication) a comparably tyrannical figure, Cleopatra. While the *symposium* was a Greek institution, Rome had comparable venues where men bonded over food and drink, as we know from satire, and Horace exploits similarities between Greek and Rome dining practices to lend a sympotic air to scenes that might also be Roman.

An essential further point on Alcaeus, however, returns us to the name of Horace's lyric poetry. What we call the *Odes* Horace himself named *Carmina*, but both titles mean 'songs'. Alcaeus' poems were composed for singing, and were sung at the *symposium*: 'lyric' is literally 'lyre-ic', poetry sung to the accompaniment of a stringed instrument. Rome did not have the same song culture, and Horace's lyrics, with the notable exception of the *Carmen Saeculare* (see pp. 71–5), were not written to be sung, even though they consistently claimed to be songs, and indeed in some cases have, in more recent times, been set to music. Horace's *Odes* are thus a literary re-creation of a song culture, performances on the page, and as such they eloquently document the complexities in Rome's adoption of Greek literary culture.

Horace advertises his special debt to Alcaeus in various ways. One indication is the metrical form of the 'Cleopatra Ode', Horace's favourite metre in the *Odes* and one so closely associated with the Greek poet as to bear his name: the 'alcaic stanza'. But a more explicit acknowledgement of Alcaeus' influence comes in *Odes* 1.32, where the poet addresses the lyre he *claims* to be playing (Figure 4), and in the process sketches its previous owner (3–16):

4. Athenian image of a *barbiton* or lyre on a *kylix*, drinking vessel, c. 480 BCE. Horace regularly claims in his *Odes* to be playing this instrument.

> ...come, speak a Latin
> song, my Greek lyre,
>
> first tuned by a citizen of Lesbos
> fierce in war, who still between battles,
> or if he had tied up his storm-tossed ship
> on the wet shore,
>
> would sing of Bacchus and the Muses
> and Venus and the boy who always clings
> to her, and Lycus lovely with his jet-black eyes
> and jet-black hair.

Horace captures Alcaeus' versatility, a politically engaged poet in violent times (the 'storm-tossed ship' alludes to poems, imitated by Horace in *Odes* 1.14, in which he used the image of the troubled Ship of State) whose poetry also encompassed other, less public, concerns of the *symposium*. Aside from this breadth of subject matter, Alcaeus offered Horace a model of poetry which, while grounded in the world of leisure, drinking sessions among friends, maintained an awareness of politics and warfare. Alcaeus and his friends were active participants in Mytilenean politics—his poetry caught them in their time away from affairs of state, and that active world is an off-stage presence also in the *Odes*. It follows in addition that lyric was another genre, to add to satire and iambus, profoundly interested in friendship, the ties that bind men together, that most urgent issue for Romans after decades of civil war and Horace's preoccupation throughout his career.

Alcaeus was Horace's key model, then, but there was much, much more to lyric than Alcaeus, and Horace deliberately defined his project with some strategic latitude.

Greek lyric poetry was a tradition that stretched over three centuries and across the entire Greek world from the Aegean sea to Italy, and encompassed a comparably broad range of styles, the only common factor being that it was all sung. Scholars in the Hellenistic period (after the death of Alexander the Great in 323 BCE) had systematized this unwieldy poetic genre into a definitive canon of nine lyric poets (and indeed given it the name 'lyric'). Even among these nine there is a vast range, but a useful division, artificial but apparently recognizable to Horace and his contemporaries, can be drawn between 'choral' and 'monodic' lyric. Choral lyric, composed by poets like Pindar and Simonides, was performed by choirs and had a more public and impressive character; it was also associated with more elaborate and variable metrical systems. Monodic lyric was associated with the *symposium* and private gatherings, and simpler metres. In metrical terms Horace associates himself exclusively with the monodic poets, the most important in the *Odes* being Alcaeus, closely followed by Sappho, a woman poet contemporary with Alcaeus and also from Mytilene on the island of Lesbos, and Anacreon. But while monodic lyric, and Alcaeus in particular, is the centre of gravity of Horace's lyric, all of these nine lyric poets feature somewhere in the *Odes*, and choral lyric is explored as a model in the fourth book especially.

In the opening poem of the *Odes*, addressing Maecenas (to whom the collection was thus effectively dedicated), Horace expresses his aspirations for his collection. He hopes that the Muses will not withhold from him the 'lyre of Lesbos', the poetic inspiration of Alcaeus and his fellow countrywoman, Sappho. But the poem also implies an even higher ambition, that he be added as an equal to the canon of the nine greatest lyric poets, a list to which by definition there could be no additions, or even that he might capture the entire Greek lyric tradition within his own Latin collection. At the opening of his collection he plays pointedly with the number nine, using nine different metres in consecutive poems, 1.1–9, to imply his control of the tradition. The boldness of his ambitions, stated or implied, can hardly be overstated. In setting out to give Rome a lyric poetry to call its own, Horace was not entirely without precedent, notably the poet Catullus a generation before, but there was nothing comparable to Horace's wholesale transfer of lyric themes and forms to Latin.

It is worth adding that Horace's statements of literary ambition or achievement still tend to be shot through with irony, ambiguity, and humour—even his overtly triumphant claim at the end of the three-book collection, 'I have wrought a monument more lasting than bronze' (3.30.1), has notes of self-deflation. Here in his first poem, the parting image of Horace, having achieved his place in the lyric canon, banging his 'exalted head on the stars' is another such moment.

After all this detailed backround, an essential question remains to be faced: what a Horatian ode is. What it isn't is a lot of things generally associated with 'lyric': Horace 'does not meditate or introspect but exhorts, questions, invites, consoles, prays and orders', in the words of Margaret Hubbard and Robin Nisbet. Typically, an ode of Horace defines a particular occasion and addresses a character, supposedly present to the poet, within it, with a view to influencing that addressee. The mottos that persist from Horace's *Odes* tend to be instructions or exhortations: *carpe diem* ('Pluck the day'), *nil desperandum* ('Do not despair'), *dulce et decorum est pro patria mori* ('It is sweet and honourable to die for one's country'), as well as *nunc est bibendum*. The figures addressed may be individuals, sometimes recognizably historical, and sometimes literary associates of the poet, a less defined group (as in the drinking companions of the 'Cleopatra Ode'), or an inanimate object like the lyre of 1.32. A special category of addressee is a god in one of Horace's numerous hymns. Other poems are directed at fictional characters, and sometimes Horace's poems will have no defined target at all.

Not the least interesting of these categories are the identifiable Romans. Maecenas is a regular presence, and features especially at important junctures, poems at the beginning, middle, and end of books; but alongside Maecenas, poems are addressed to a spectrum of elite public figures, who for Horace's first readers would have looked like a representative sweep of elite Rome: names like Sestius, Munatius Plancus, Agrippa, Asinius Pollio, Sallustius Crispus, Dellius, Licinius Murena, and Messalla Corvinus evoke public figures who, crucially, had not necessarily seen eye-to-eye during the Civil Wars. L. Sestius, for instance, was another figure who had fought 'on the wrong side' at the battle of Philippi, and he continued to celebrate unapologetically the memory of his commander Marcus Brutus. It was for this very reason that Augustus made him consul in his own place, after he himself had stepped down, in 23 BCE, a strikingly conciliatory gesture. (Sestius' prominence in the collection, addressed in *Odes* 1.4, points to its date of publication, 23 BCE.) But these men who had been fighting each other not so long before are all, in the *Odes*, gathered together in Horace's literary *symposium*, *sodales* drinking each other's health. The message again is the restoration of *amicitia*, friendship, the relations critical to the functioning of Roman society that years of civil war had shattered almost beyond repair.

Augustus himself is never a 'guest' at Horace's *symposium*, as if bringing him down to this level would puncture his mystique. (In the fourth book he is addressed, but as a transcendent, protective force, not a fellow drinker.) But it is worth considering another presence. As we read the *Odes*, we may adopt the perspective of the poetic voice, or of the addressee, and the common reception of Horace by his readers as a wise counsellor and friend suggests the latter is as natural an impulse. Either way, we the readers also participate in Horace's convivial Roman gathering, and this makes Horace's lyric poetry by design an engine for peace and social order encompassing the whole of the Roman upper classes, so recently at each other's throats.

How far Horace's poems to individual Romans can be shaped by their character and interests, in sometimes quite challenging ways, is worth observing. The poem that addresses Sestius, whose family (as we know from archaeological evidence) ran industrial operations producing amphorae and bricks, moves from a celebration of spring to a meditation on life's brevity, but imagery of manufacture, the *officinae*, 'factories', of the Cyclopes reopening their operations after a winter break, playfully alludes to the Sestius family business.

There is a more tendentious address in one of Horace's most celebrated poems (2.10, on the theme of moderation). From this poem comes our expression 'Golden Mean', translating *aurea mediocritas*, although Horace's formulation is a more arresting oxymoron, a mundane middlingness, *mediocritas*, which is yet as precious as gold, *aurea*. It is no coincidence either, though it is rather wonderful, that 2.10 sits at the middle of the middle book of the collection of *Odes* 1–3. The addressee of the poem is 'Licinius', and while we cannot be certain, it is likely that he is Licinius Murena, a brother-in-law of Maecenas. Murena was notorious for his unrestrained tongue, and at the time of the publication of *Odes* 1–3 was embarked on a sequence of missteps which would eventually lead to his execution after a conspiracy against Augustus. Murena favoured the Peripatetic philosophy of Aristotle, and it is the importance of the recognizably Peripatetic principle of the middle way that Horace is impressing upon him. It seems that there was nothing abstract about his advice.

Horace's lyric poems are short, rarely over seventy lines, and typically much shorter, and while certain themes recur they are essentially self-contained. Capturing the full variety of Horace's lyric verse would be impossible at any length, but there can be no adequate introduction that doesn't consider at least one poem in some detail.

Odes 2.7 is a welcome home for a long-lost comrade:

> O Pompeius, many times in my company drawn
> to the edge of disaster under Brutus' command,
>   who is it that has made you a private citizen again
>   and restored you to your ancestral gods and the Italian sky,

foremost of my drinking companions, with whom   5
many a time I broke off the sluggish day with neat wine,
   garlanded and my hair sleek
      with Syrian malobathrum?

In your company I experienced Philippi and swift retreat,
my little shield left improperly behind me,   10
   when virtue was broken and aggressors
      touched the demeaning earth with their chins.

But I was snatched away in a cloud by swift Mercury
in my terror through the enemy;
   you the wave sucked back into war   15
      and swept you along seething straits.

So pay back to Jupiter the feast that you vowed,
and lay down your body weary with campaigning
   under my laurel tree, and give no quarter
      to the casks of wine I have kept back for you.   20

Fill to the brim smooth Egyptian cups
with forgetful Massic, pour perfumed oils
   from brimming shells. Who will hurry
      to weave garlands of moist celery

or of myrtle? Who will Venus call the master   25
of drinking? I shall run as wild as Edonian
   Bacchanals. How sweet it is
      to lose my mind in welcoming back a friend!

Pompeius (we know nothing more about him, but his name evokes
Pompey the Great, his son Sextus Pompey, and past conflict) had
fought alongside Horace at Philippi in 42 BCE, but unlike Horace
he had persisted in his opposition to Augustus, probably joining
Sextus Pompey and then Mark Antony in Egypt. Now at length,
however, he is back in Rome, and the answer to the question of
who was responsible for his amnesty is of course Augustus

himself, the indirectness of the praise of the emperor typical of *Odes* 1–3, at least.

This lyric poem features not one *symposium* but several, evoking the drinking sessions of Horace's and Pompeius' youth as comrades on campaign as well as the celebration of Pompeius' return that is the occasion of the poem. There are subtle contrasts between now and then, an exotic quality to those past carousals, and divine endorsement of the current one, fulfilling as it does Pompeius' vow to Jupiter. But the bond between these two men is emphasized throughout, words for friendship and commonality proliferating, subtle repetition of me/my, you/your underlying the continuity of their relationship through all the vicissitudes of their lives. The *symposium* fosters friendship, here a friendship that buries civil war, and lyric is its privileged expression.

Also characteristically lyric here is the perspective on the passage of time. Horace addresses from middle age the behaviour of his youth. Much of the character of Horace's *Odes* derives from this self-positioning of the poet as a man in his late thirties and forties, which is true both to the Greek lyric tradition and to Horace's actual age in the 20s BCE. The hard-earned experience of an older man licenses Horace to offer the life guidance with which the *Odes* is perhaps most associated, and also shapes the view of love affairs that we find here, areas I shall shortly pursue in a little more depth. In the context of this poem it allows for an acknowledgement of peace set effectively against the backdrop of relentless war.

But while overtly political, 2.7 is also representative for its self-awareness as a poem in a complex literary tradition. Horace's overarching debt is to the lyric poets, broadly defined, and the reference in line 10 to losing his shield at Philippi is less a historical detail than a mark of literary affiliation: Alcaeus, Anacreon, and Archilochus had all described mislaying their shields in flight from an enemy, and one effect was to distinguish their poetry and poetic personas from the heroic ethos of martial epic, the higher literary form associated with Homer (and in Rome with the *Aeneid* that Virgil was in the process of writing). Horace's lyric thus simultaneously advertises itself as a less ambitious literary form and celebrates the quieter virtues of peace over the glamour of war. The association that Horace forges between his lyric verse and the peace achieved by Augustus' victory in the Civil Wars persists to the end, as we shall see.

Reinforcing the association of the short poems of Horace's *Odes* with a lighter poetics is an allusion to the leading poet of the Hellenistic age, Callimachus, whose principles of literary value—a preference for short, refined poetry over grand epics—Horace can claim to honour even while imitating poets from long before him, here as in the *Epodes*. Here Horace's reminiscence of breaking off the day with drink recalls what is perhaps in modern times Callimachus' most famous poem (*Epigram* 34; *Anthologia Palatina* 7.80), translated by William Cory as beginning, 'They told me, Heraclitus, they told me you were dead, | They brought me bitter news to hear and bitter tears to shed. | I wept as I remember'd how often you and I | Had tired the sun with talking and sent him down the sky'. Again we have to appreciate the sophisticated assertions of literary affiliation that these reminiscences of predecessors encode, but understand also that they in no way compromise, indeed rather they enrich, a skilled poet's expression of authentic human experience. Unlike Heraclitus, Pompeius is, against all expectations, alive!

A final thought on brevity, the highly restrictive forms—short poems, but also miniature stanzas—to which Horace in his lyric poetry commits himself: there are, by way of illustration, thirty-eight words in my translation of the first stanza of 2.7, and eighteen in the Latin original; and my words don't conform to a metrical scheme generated within, and hitherto restricted to, the Greek language. Concise expression that does not surrender clarity is perhaps Horace's most remarkable achievement in this poetry, and one means of achieving it was a precision in word selection. An example in this poem is the Latin word in line 3 that I have translated as 'private citizen', *Quiritem*, a word that for Romans evoked an emotive cocktail of belonging, antiquity, peace, and constitutional order. *Malobathrum* in line 8 is an exotic word for an exotic thing, a spice whose name derives from the Indian Sanskrit *tamalapattram*, 'leaf of the tamala tree'. But how better than with such an elusive, evocative word to convey not just places far away from 'the Italian sky', and exotic substances with nostalgia-inducing aromas, but also experiences mistily recalled from a distant, irrecoverable youth?

If peace is Horatian lyric's natural circumstance, time is its great problematic (another inheritance from the Greeks), the thing most thoroughly and damagingly beyond our control and hence most in need of philosophical management. The perspective is again that of the middle-aged man, newly alert to the inevitability of his death. Poem 3.29, a powerful and memorable restatement of core themes appropriate to the second-last poem of the first collection—indeed it is widely considered among the greatest of all Horace's compositions; John Dryden translated it, for instance—can illustrate both the guidance that Horace offers and the manner in which he conveys it. On another poem, the fine (and splendidly acerbic) scholar David West commented: 'Some scholars have marked the poem down as a tissue of commonplaces, which it is. Like the music of Mozart.' There is never much that is very revolutionary about Horace's ethical advice, but his expression of it is superlative, and it repays close attention.

Horace addresses Maecenas, and invites him to leave the city and its political concerns ('what Tartary is plotting, and Balkh ruled by Cyrus, | and the chaotic Don') for a spell and join Horace to drink. But the sympotic imperative to throw aside one's cares and get drunk modulates into a deeper meditation on events and our limited control of them, and then the proper way to deal with human limitation, by living in the present moment (3.29.29–64):

With his knowledge of future time, God buries
what is to come in impenetrable night,   30
   and laughs if a mortal is more anxious
      than he should be. Remember

to deal calmly with what is at hand. Everything else
flows like a river, now in mid-channel
   gliding peacefully down to the Tuscan   35
      sea, now rolling along

eroded rocks, uprooted treetrunks, cattle, houses
all together, with a roar from the mountains
   and the trees on its banks,
      as the wild flood stirs up   40

the peaceful stream. That man will be in command
of his life, and happy, who can say
   every day, 'I have lived'. Tomorrow let
      the Father fill the sky with black cloud

or clear sunlight, but he will not render   45
null and void whatever is behind us, nor
   misshape or make unmade
      what once the fleeing hour has brought.

Fortune enjoys her cruel business and
stubbornly pursuing her arrogant game   50
   reassigns her fickle honours,
      now favouring me, now another.

I praise her while she stays. But if she shakes out
her swift wings, I pay back what she gave me,
   wrap myself in my virtue and woo   55
      honest Poverty, bringing no dowry.

It is not my way, if the mast moans
with African gales, to resort to
   desperate pleas, or to bargain with prayers
      that my Cyprian and Tyrian merchandise   60

not augment the riches of the greedy sea.
When that happens, safe in the protection
of a two-oared dinghy the breeze and the protector gods
of sailors will carry me through the Aegean storms.

The philosophy is clear here, and partly so because a simple prescription for happiness is expressed in simple language. The language of lyric is more refined than the everyday speech typical of satire or iambus, but Greek monodic lyric used a register close to vernacular language, and Horace can, when it is appropriate, be very plain. Another effect still evident in my English version is the flow of sense units from stanza to stanza when the subject is everything in life that one cannot control, the image of a river in flood.

A further, very beautiful piece of composition is harder to explain as it involves the metrical form of the poem: 3.29 is in Alcaeus' signature metre, alcaics, and an inherent dynamic of the alcaic stanza is the slow, stretched quality of every third line, lacking a pause that is observed in the middle of the first two lines. Words of particular weight thus tend to be set in this third line. A good example in this poem is line 55, where the Latin words *mea | uirtute me inuoluo*, 'I wrap myself in my virtue', are set in such a way that *m'inuoluo* (the words coalesce very effectively as he wraps himself tightly), describing the action of wrapping a cloak around himself, gains special emphasis from placement in the middle of the third line. In line 43 the composition is even more subtle. Horace sets the word *uīxī*, 'I have lived', in the third line again, but in such a way that the anticipated expansion is not realized: it is followed by the pause normally only expected in the first two lines. The effect is to isolate the word momentarily, and since 'I have lived', by Horace's argument, is the only thing that ever requires saying, the versification offers exquisite support to the moral.

Line 55 is a good illustration also of the density of texture required by Horace's quest for brevity—lucid expression within restrictive metrical forms, the 'little strophes' of Sappho and Alcaeus that a contemporary critic, Dionysius of Halicarnassus, described (*De Compositione Verborum* 19) and which made Horace, perforce, a miniaturist in words. Quintilian offers a succinct assessment of Horace's lyric verse (10.1.96): 'Horace can rise in register sometimes', he says, 'and yet he is also full of agreeableness and charm, creative in his figures of speech, and daring to most felicitous effect in his choice of words'. In this case it is both a figure of speech and an exquisite choice of word. With *mea | uirtute me inuoluo* Horace has turned from his account of human happiness to describe how he himself meets ill fortune when he encounters it. Virtue becomes a warm garment that protects him against the chill winds of misfortune, but ancient readers would recognize something more specific evoked in the combination of virtue and a cloak in the context of poverty: a philosopher from the Cynic school, known for their rigorous commitment to virtue as the only source of happiness, and rejection of any possession beyond a staff, a bowl, and a single cloak wrapped double to keep out the cold.

The philosophical position of Horace in the *Odes*, though often tending to Epicureanism and a quietist Epicurean retreat from public life into 'the Garden', is eclectic. What we see in this poem, as regularly through the *Odes*, is Horace asserting a moral value, that of simple living, which, while an ideal shared by more than one philosophy, was also a Roman ideal related to their myth of origin among hardy peasants. At times the aesthetic principles of the *Odes*—small poems, humble aspirations—align closely with their ethical principles—virtue grounded in humility and moderation, often exemplified by Horace's villa, which he insists was modest in dimension, and was located in the Sabine country east of Rome, a space in itself associated by Romans with old-fashioned decency and thrift.

At the beginning of the third book of *Odes* a series of six poems sharing the same metre as well as a very loose thematic unity and a moralistic and nationalistic emphasis (they are called in modern scholarship the 'Roman Odes') also tend to ground their moral vision in this ideal of virtuous simplicity. In the first 'Roman Ode', 3.1, Horace deploys as a foil to his own simple existence in his 'Sabine valley' a rich man of unlimited desires, who even extends his sea-side villa into the sea. He is described as *dominus terrae || fastidiosus*, 'the owner disdainful of dry land'. In the Latin, the word for 'of dry land', *terrae*, is at the end of one stanza, and that for 'disdainful of' at the beginning of the next.

Here we can bring in another ancient testimony on Horace's *Odes*, a character in Petronius' *Satyricon* (108), not the most obvious place to find acute literary criticism, who nevertheless very accurately credits Horace with *curiosa felicitas*, 'meticulous felicity', the *mot juste* painstakingly identified. There are moments in Horace's lyric poetry where a perfectly chosen word is perfectly combined with another word and perfectly located; and here in 3.1 we are looking at just such a moment. *Fastidiosus*, translated 'disdainful of', is richer than that. It means full of a psychological state called *fastidium*. The *-osus* ending is also found in Petronius' *curiosus*, 'care-ful', Horace's descriptions of the river Hydaspes (p. 2) as *fabulosus*, full of fables, and his teacher Orbilius as *plagosus*, full of blows. *Fastidium* meanwhile is closest to disgust: it is what you would feel, to borrow an example from Pliny the Elder, if you were contemplating having to eat a lizard (*Historia Naturalis* 30.90). A fine word, then, which is combined with another, *terrae*, to create a paradox, a human sensibility so absurdly refined that it is filled with revulsion for the natural human habitat of dry land.

But the placement! 'Dry land' and 'disgusted' are separated by empty space on the page, or by the requisite pause between stanzas in a spoken recitation. (We know that ancient poetic texts marked divisions between stanzas, if not by space on the page, at least by a symbol called a *paragraphos*.) The very word *fastidiosus* is thus maintaining its fastidious distance from the mainland. Horace talks in the *Ars Poetica* of a 'clever combination' that takes familiar words and makes them new (47–8), something modern critics call *ostranenie* or defamiliarization, and he certainly exemplifies his own injunction here.

Lyric poetry considers itself to be love poetry. But the character of love in lyric is idiosyncratic, and shaped by the matter of age raised earlier. An illustration is *Odes* 3.10, which adopts a scenario—the poet locked out of his lover's house, lying pitifully on the threshold, and begging to be admitted—that was especially associated with love elegy, a form of love poetry written by Horace's contemporaries Tibullus, Propertius, and Ovid. Elegy documented a young man's love life: as Ovid wrote, 'An aged soldier is a disgrace, a disgrace an aged lover' (*Amores* 1.9.4). The lyric lover, by contrast, is a middle-aged man, and while most of this poem follows a conventional script, Horace signs off with a warning that, unlike a young lover, he is not going to hang around indefinitely: 'This body of mine will not endure for ever your threshold and the waters from heaven' (19–20). The word translated 'body' here, *latus*, literally 'flank', can imply sexual capacity, and the sentence as a whole leaves it open whether it is the physical shortcomings of a middle-aged man that will cut short his vigil, or the different mental attitude of an older man who really can't be bothered. The woman addressed in this poem is called Lyce (her name, like the names of other lovers, is potentially significant, suggesting a 'wolf' in Greek), and we shall meet her again.

Odes 3.26 is another love poem, but in its depiction of the poet as on the point of retiring from the life of love it captures both lyric's awareness of ageing, that the lover may well be too old for the game, and the position of this poem very close to the end of the collection: giving up love is tantamount to giving up lyric. A mark of retirement was to dedicate the tools of your profession to an

appropriate god. Here the lover, humorously equated with a
retiring soldier, dedicates to Venus the equipment that might
achieve access to a lover's house, a lyre or a crowbar. We are not
quite at the end of the book, though, and in an ironic conclusion
the poet unexpectedly begs for just one more opportunity:

> Up to now I have lived fit for girls,
> and I have campaigned not without honour.
>> Now my equipment and my lyre, discharged
>>> from war, will hang on this wall
>
> which guards the left side of sea-born Venus.
> Here, here, offer up the bright
>> tapers and crowbars and axes
>>> that threatened resistant doors.
>
> O goddess, ruler of wealthy Cyprus and
> Memphis that never knows Thracian snow,
>> O queen, with upraised lash
>>> flick conceited Chloe, just the once.

There is some productive ambiguity as to precisely which wall he
is pinning these items to. The temple of Venus on the Capitoline
was flanked on its immediate left by the shrine of Mens, Sanity,
a most appropriate point of call for a recovered lover. Is Horace
in the temple of the love goddess, or in recovery next door? In
its very ambiguity the poem captures the anxieties of the
late-lyric lover.

In Horace's love poetry, Lyce and Chloe are joined by Lyde, Lalage,
Leuconoe, and many other women: 'Lalage', to illustrate an earlier
point, speaks and smiles delightfully (1.22.23–4), and her name
suggests 'chatterbox'. The lyric lover claims the wisdom of
experience, and unlike the elegiac lover, eternally committed to a
single woman, knows that every affair is temporary. But if lyric
love is not monogamous, that doesn't mean it lacks intensity:

Odes 2.8 is a powerful account of Barine's sexual magnetism, for instance, while in 1.19 *in me tota ruens Venus | Cyprum deseruit*, 'Venus deserts Cyprus and in full strength overwhelms me'. *Odes* 1.30 is a love poem that is also, like 3.26, an example of another common lyric type, a hymn addressed to a god, in this case Venus. But it is the intervention of Horace's special patron Mercury, whose name *Mercuriusque* fills the final line (implying the fulfilment of the god's epiphany), that will prove decisive:

> O Venus, queen of Cnidus and Paphos,
> spurn your beloved Cyprus and move
> to the gorgeous shrine of Glycera, who is calling you
> with clouds of incense.
>
> Your passionate boy must hurry along with you,
> and the Graces and Nymphs with their girdles loosened,
> and Youth, less charming without you,
> and Mercury.

* * *

Some years after his first collection of *Odes* Horace would return with a fourth, an intriguing advance on its predecessor. In between came the composition and performance of the *Carmen Saeculare*, 'Song of the Century', which, while also a hymn and even sharing the same metrical form as 1.30, sapphics (named after Alcaeus' much more famous contemporary on Lesbos, Sappho), is in other respects a dramatic departure from Horace's previous lyric poetry.

The *Carmen Saeculare* is Horace's only lyric that was composed to be sung, and, performed by two separate choruses of the ritually significant number of twenty-seven girls and twenty-seven boys, all born of parents still living, it formed an integral part of what must have been the most impressive public event of the Augustan age. From 31 May to 3 June 17 BCE, Rome marked the *Ludi Saeculares* or Secular Games, a religious festival that in theory recurred only once in the maximum extent of a human lifetime: the *saeculum* of its title was a span of 110 years. Secular Games were not games in our sense, but a ceremony that had originated in the crisis of Rome's conflict with Carthage two centuries before, a ritual designed to expiate ominous prodigies. For the games in 17 BCE, we have surviving a detailed record of the event inscribed on stone, rediscovered as recently as 1890, in which 'Q. Horatius Flaccus' is confirmed as the author of the climactic hymn (Figure 1), and we also have a Sibylline oracle, the mysterious pronouncement from which Augustus and his fellow *quindecimviri* (the Fifteen Men, a priestly college) had extracted divine guidance for the staging of the ceremony, including the instruction that 'Latin hymns' be sung.

The upshot is what looks to us like a characteristically Augustan concoction, a festival of intensely contemporary significance clothed in the associations of hoary antiquity. In particular, a ritual originally designed to mollify gods of the underworld was repurposed as an appeal for future prosperity, an elaborate programme of sacrifices proclaiming the inauguration of a new and better age.

Extending over three nights and days, the Games culminated in offerings to the twin siblings Apollo and Diana on the third day, twenty-seven ritual cakes presented to each deity by Augustus and his son-in-law and anointed heir Marcus Agrippa. These gods, particularly cultivated by Augustus, functioned as the conceptual linchpin of proceedings, drawing the various observances across the three days into a coherent message of national renewal. Horace's Latin paean (as a hymn to Apollo or Artemis was known) reflects these dynamics, delivering a message of rebirth, fertility, and peace that was also embodied in the young choristers who sang it and the perpetually youthful deities to whom it was addressed (1–8):

O Phoebus Apollo and Diana, patron of forests,
Radiant glory of heaven, always worshipped
and to be worshipped, grant what we pray for
in this holy moment,

when the Sibylline verses have bidden
chosen girls and pure boys
to sing a song to the gods who love
the seven hills.

In style the *Carmen Saeculare* is markedly different from Horace's
other lyric verse. Its word order is more straightforward, the
thought and syntax simpler, and the language at times strikingly
prosaic. The sapphic metre (Figure 5) has been adapted by Horace
in ways that are best explained as making the rhythm more readily
apparent to its young singers. The metre itself brought to the
Carmen an air of domesticity inherited from Sappho, understood
by the Romans at least as a poet specially concerned with

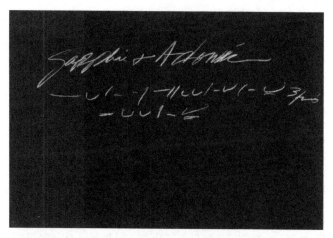

5. **Detail from Cy Twombly, *8 odi di Orazio*, which depicts the scheme
of the sapphic stanza, one of Horace's favourite metrical systems in
the *Odes*.**

marriage—all associations congruent with the larger message of social renewal. When Horace looks back at the *Carmen* in his fourth book of *Odes* he addresses one of the girl choristers significantly as a future bride (4.6.41–4):

> Soon, when married, you will say, 'I performed
> when the *saeculum* brought round again the festal days
> a song welcome to the gods, trained in the measures
> of Horace the bard.'

What Horace had forged in the *Carmen* was a medium geared to the peculiar demands of live performance within an ideologically charged ceremony. Alliteration, assonance, and repetition of related forms (polyptoton is the technical term) encourage conceptual links between the disparate threads in play, for instance between Augustus' marriage legislation, *decreta* (18), and the 'fixed' (*certus*; 21) cosmic order that measures out 110 years between Secular Games, creating a dense, rich, but comprehensible encapsulation of the constellation of ideas feeding into Augustus' celebration of Rome's new epoch. Furthermore, while Virgil's *Aeneid*, very recently published, had established a potent national myth of origin that informs the hymn profoundly, the *Carmen* is simpler in literary texture, not alluding to Alcaeus or Callimachus but instead guiding the eyes of its listeners to the monuments of the city around them. Horace's hymn was performed twice on the third day, before the Temple of Apollo on the Palatine hill, dedicated by Augustus to his patron deity, and then before the Temple of Jupiter Optimus Maximus on the Capitoline, the centre of Roman religious observance.

Perhaps the most arresting aspect of the *Carmen* is the way that it opens by appealing for divine favour in a project of national renewal, but concludes by enacting its own efficacy. By the end of the song the poet is not so much requesting the gods' endorsement as describing it in action (61–72):

Phoebus Apollo, prophet graced
with the shining bow, and dear to the nine Muses
who relieves with his health-giving skill
the body's tired limbs,

if he looks with favour on the altars on the Palatine
extends Rome's and prosperous Latium's existence
for a further cycle and into an ever more
better age,

and Diana, mistress of the Aventine and Algidus,
cherishes the prayers of the Fifteen Men
and lends friendly ears to the prayers
of the children.

As such Horace's Secular Song alerts us to ancient perceptions
of the potency of language. It is good to remind ourselves that
this was a culture which believed that verbal formulations, if
expertly designed, had the power even to persuade the highest
beings, or as magic to reshape the world, and to ponder what
ambitions Horace might have harboured for his other poetry
and its capacity to mould its environment. That is a thought to
balance against the habitual irony of Horace's statements of
poetic achievement, and to bear in mind as we contemplate his
return to lyric in *Odes* 4.

* * *

'Wars long suspended, Venus, | you wage anew. Spare me, I beg,
I beg of you' (4.1–2), begins the first poem of the new book. To be
in love and to write lyric poetry, as we know, are synonymous, and
Horace was back in harness: the first poem of Sappho's Hellenistic
edition, a hymn to Aphrodite, is an important point of reference,
and for the ancients Sappho was the greatest of love poets. How
long it was after the publication of books 1–3 in 23 BCE that book 4
emerged is a matter of debate, but a broad consensus places it
around 13 BCE. What is not in doubt is that Horace, as was his

wont, makes a theme of his own advancing age. The opening address to Venus continues (4–8):

> Cease, cruel
>
> mother of sweet Cupids,
>> to twist a man hardened to your soft
> commands around his fiftieth year. Away with you
>> to where the seductive prayers of young men summon you.

The problem of age, central to the middle-aged aesthetic of *Odes* 1–3, is in book 4 urgent, and the result is some deeply moving verse such as his address to his lover Phyllis at the close of 4.11, a poem celebrating the birthday of Maecenas, the only appearance of Horace's patron and friend in a book which is more directly concerned with the emperor and his family than his previous lyric (31–6):

> Come now, the very last
> of my love affairs,
>
> (henceforth I shall not feel passion
> for any other woman), learn well measures to sing
> with your lovely voice. Black anxieties
> will be lessened by song.

More challenging is 4.13, a brutal attack on a former lover, Lyce, that recalls some of the worst misogyny of the *Epodes* (1–12):

> The gods have heard my prayers, Lyce, the
> gods, Lyce, have heard me: you are old, and yet
>> you wish to appear beautiful
>> and you misbehave and drink too much
>
> and, half-cut, accost unwilling Cupid
> with quavering voice. But he stands guard
>> on the lovely cheeks of Chia,
>> who is youthful, and clever with the lyre.

There are less aggressive notes as the poem develops ('What do you preserve of her, of her, | who breathed loves, who stole me from myself'; 18–20) which direct our attention to Horace's own ageing, and we may recall that it was outside the same Lyce's door that the middle-aged Horace was grumpily reclining in *Odes* 3.10. If Lyce is old, Horace is yet older, and the aggression necessarily self-directed, in part at least, in the context of a book obsessed with the passage of time: the boy Ligurinus, an object of passion in 4.1, is confronted with the ineluctability of ageing in 4.10. Meanwhile 4.7 is a spring poem that modulates into a meditation on life's brevity ('Have no hope for immortality, warns the year | and the hour that snatches away the life-giving day', 7–8), and as such is often compared to a poem with a similar theme, 1.4 to Sestius. But 4.7 is the darker composition, its emphasis more on death and less on carousing as its best antidote. Here also time is weighing more heavily.

Other preoccupations of the first collection also appear in intensified form in book 4, and as a shorter, single-book collection we can also more easily gain a sense of the lyric book as a whole. While favouring the monodic poetry of Alcaeus, Sappho, and Anacreon as primary models, Horace had reserved for himself the option of exploiting the whole capacious category of Greek lyric, and there were Pindaric moments in the earlier collection. But *Odes* 4 operates more consistently in that higher register, where models might be Simonides as well as Pindar, and even the epic poets, Homer, Ennius, and Virgil. Augustus is addressed directly for the first time in 4.5, albeit in highly complimentary terms, while 4.4 is a celebration of the military successes of Drusus and Tiberius, the stepsons of Augustus and the latter his ultimate successor, over the Vindelici and other tribes in the Alps, which opens with a long, sweeping sentence, including a parenthesis expressing ignorance of a point of detail, that is all very reminiscent of Pindar's style. Poem 4.14 addresses the same campaign, and the theme suits the general air of finality that Horace lends this book. That campaign in the Alps was claimed

6. The Tropaeum Alpium at La Turbie on the heights above Monaco, a monument dedicated to Augustus by the Senate and People of Rome. It marked the final conquest of the Alps that formed Italy's northern and north-western border and the completion of Augustus' project to restore order to Italy. As such it echoes one message of Horace's fourth book of *Odes*.

by Augustus to have set the seal on the peace that he had brought not just to Rome but to the entire Italian peninsula, the mountain barrier of the Alps marking Italy's northern boundary. An Augustan monument that still survives at La Turbie (Figure 6), on the heights above Monaco, the Trophy of the Alps (La Turbie derives its name from the Latin *Trophaeum*), bore a similar message of geopolitical completion achieved by the pacification of the mountains.

Horace is stretching the capacities of his lyric, then, but still within limits. The metre of both poems on Drusus and Tiberius is the alcaic stanza, a metre that Horace prefers for his more solemn compositions, but which is still a monodic form. *Odes* 4.2 embodies the tension, a poem that explicitly contemplates Pindar as a model for praising Augustus, but rejects the model for himself and passes the task to his addressee, Iullus Antonius (a poet and the son of Mark Antony, raised by his stepmother, Augustus' sister, in Rome). The lightest possible metre, sapphics, corroborates Horace's self-image here, but equally Augustus gets the Pindaric praise he deserves. The final poem of book 4, as we shall see, reasserts in another way its humble status, but again so as to reinforce a claim about Augustus' (and Horace's) achievements.

An attempt to explain the higher aspirations (always according to ancient notions of literary significance) represented by book 4, and the poems on Tiberius and Drusus particularly, is found in the ancient life of Horace:

> As for his writings, [Augustus] rated them so highly, and was so convinced that they would survive for ever, that he engaged him to compose not only the *Carmen Saeculare* but also the triumph of Tiberius and Drusus, his stepsons, over the Vindelici, and consequently obliged him to add a fourth to his three books of *Odes* after a long intervening time.

This is not how we generally assume that Horace's poetry came to be, but what is very discernible in the book is Horace's enhanced status after the *Carmen Saeculare*, a commission that established him as in effect the national poet. He returns to the performance of the *Carmen* in 4.6, as we have seen, but other poems, 4.8 and 4.9, boast of his poetry's power, proven in his first lyric collection, to immortalize its subjects (4.8 adopts the metre shared by the first and last poems of *Odes* 1–3, making it a claim for his lyric poetry as a whole), while 4.3 offers thanks to Melpomene, Muse of song (21–4):

> This is all of your doing,
>> That I am pointed out by the finger of passers-by
> as the player of the Roman lyre.
>> That I breathe and please, if I do please, is your gift.

The final poem of the fourth book of Horace's lyric oeuvre, and perhaps of his poetic career, seeks to confirm Horace's status as Rome's laureate. *Odes* 4.15 celebrates the peace that Augustus has given Rome (17–24):

> While Caesar stands guard over the world, no madness
> between citizens or violence will drive out peace,
>   nor anger that hammers swords into shape
>   and brings suffering towns to blows.
>
> Those who drink the deep Danube
> will not break the Julian laws, nor the Getae,
>   nor the Chinese or untrustworthy Persians,
>   nor those born by the river Don.

But that peace will find its expression in the most lyric of activities, drinking and song. Furthermore the poem begins with an imitation of an influential passage in Callimachus which had in turn inspired Latin versions by Virgil and Propertius, and was a well-established way of defining the lower aspirations of one's poetry, as compared with epic especially (1–4):

> Apollo on his lyre, when I wished to speak of battles
> and conquered cities, protested with me
>   that I must not spread my narrow sails
>   over the Tyrrhenian sea.

Horace is forbidden by Apollo to write epic, the poetry of war, but there is no call for poets of war now that Augustus has established peace across the world. Lyric has found its ideal subject in a city and empire at peace. Or to turn that around, Augustan Rome has become what Horace's *Odes* have striven to make it, by the power of his poetry: a lyric space.

Chapter 5
Epistles

The *Odes* had taken an entire, complex tradition of Greek poetry
and reinvented it in Roman form, a momentous achievement.
With the first book of *Epistles*, a collection of poetic letters
published three years after *Odes* 1–3 in 20–19 BCE, Horace
returned to the kind of poetry that he had insisted was not really
poetry at all, 'conversations' like the *Satires* back at the start of his
career. In form and style they advertise that kinship, with the
same hexametrical form as his satires, and a similarly colloquial
style of expression working against the formality of the verse
structure. Meanwhile, the philosophical reflections which are at
the heart of the *Epistles* often have close parallels in the *Odes*.
In other respects, however, Horace's *Epistles* represent a highly
innovative departure: a collection of letters in verse was
unprecedented, and Roman poetry was all about following
precedent. It is worth saying that these poems which claim to be
letters are no more real letters than the *Odes* are songs or the
Satires conversations. But Horace's evocation of the letter in
poetic form may well count as his most ingenious
accomplishment.

The first *liber Epistularum* begins with a poem addressed to
Maecenas announcing his rejection of poetry in favour of
philosophy (*Epistles* 1.10–19):

So now I'm laying aside my verses and all the other trifles.   10
What is right and proper is my concern and my target and all that
    I'm about.
I am gathering and storing what by and by I can draw on.
And if you ask me, under which leader, under whose roof I shelter,
I have no master whose words I am forced to swear by:
wherever the storm carries me, there I happily travel.   15
Sometimes I turn public-spirited and plunge into political life,
unwavering guardian and attendant of true virtue;
at other times I slip back unconsciously into the philosophy of
    Aristippus,
and try to subject the world to me, not me to the world.

Horace characterizes the kind of philosophy that his collection
will offer, and it is again eclectic: he follows no guru, and is as
happy to play at being a Stoic (the political activity of 16–17 points
to that school) as a Cyrenaic like Aristippus (an extreme hedonist).
These are philosophical polar extremes, amusingly caricatured,
but philosophy, for all Horace's evasive humour, does indeed prove
to be the preoccupation of this collection, and specifically the
question of *recte uiuere*, how to live the good life. This was the
central concern of all ancient philosophical schools, which kept
their ruminations commendably tied to the practicalities of
human existence. And Horace's philosophical pronouncements do
indeed resist dogmatic allegiance to any particular school, albeit
with a general inclination towards Epicureanism, a philosophy
that advocated retirement from public life.

Horace's statement of philosophical independence in line 14,
Nullius addictus iurare in uerba magistri, was adapted by the
Royal Society in their motto *Nullius in uerba*, 'Take no-one's word
for it', and we see a hint here again of the personal character that
Horace had begun to lend to the core Roman principle of *libertas*,
'freedom', in the *Satires*. Also reminiscent of satire is the colloquial
style he adopts. Line 11 in Latin, *quid uerum'tque decens curo't*

rogo't omnis in hoc sum, jams words together and hobbles the
line cadence in such a way as to make poetry seem like prose, an
artful illustration of the retirement from artful writing that he
is announcing. In line 12, the Latin verbs I have translated
'gathering and storing' (*condo et compono*) are well-established
metaphorical terms for writing poetry, which Horace here
meaningfully restores to their basic, practical meanings.

Letters and philosophy are a good match, and not only because
letters, as an intimate form of communication that could travel
long distances, were in antiquity an established medium for
sharing philosophical instruction—by Epicurus the founder of
Epicureanism, for instance, or St Paul. In addition letters arriving
from Horace imply his retirement away from the hurly-burly of
everyday life to a place conducive to contemplation of the
fundamental truths of his and our existence. Often in this collection
Horace is explicitly located in the countryside, communicating
with friends from a position of (typically) calm detachment.

The most obvious way in which these poems identify themselves
as letters is their clear address of an identified recipient, Maecenas
in three of them, but otherwise a range of generally young and
up-and-coming Roman addressees. The occasions of these poems
also offer the impression of an authentic correspondence. We
have invitations (4 and 5), letters of recommendation (9) or
introduction (12), a rapid note (13) anxiously sent after someone
already on his way—varying greatly in length, tone, and register,
and implying a wider and even more various life unspoken.

But Horace also includes the conventional formulae of a letter,
greetings, and sign-offs, albeit elegantly varied and exploited. At
the end of *Epistles* 1.10, a letter to Aristius Fuscus that playfully
argues the superiority of the quiet life in the country over life in
the city, his sign-off seems casual, but is in fact richly suggestive
(1.10.49–50):

I am dictating this to you behind the crumbling shrine of Vacuna,
happy in all ways except that you are not with me.

The goddess Vacuna, a Sabine deity of victory (Horace is at his
Sabine estate), was associated both with success and (through the
Latin word *uacare*, the origin of the English 'vacation') with the
leisure and philosophical study that Horace promotes in this
poem and the wider collection. The shrine where Horace is sitting
and dictating activates thoughts also (through reminiscence of the
great Epicurean poet Lucretius, active in the 50s BCE) of an
Epicurean retreat to a place apart. (The implications of Horace's
dictation I have touched on earlier, p. 13.) Not dissimilar in the
impact of an ostensibly throwaway 'P.S.' is the conclusion of the
twelfth *Epistle*, where Horace appends a summary of current
news for a correspondent away in Sicily, as a letter naturally
would—but the day's gossip turns out to be the universal peace
and prosperity achieved by Augustus (12.25–9):

In case you haven't heard how things stand in Rome,
the valour of Agrippa has brought low the Cantabrian,
and Claudius Nero the Armenian. Phraates on bended knee
has accepted Caesar's authority. Golden Plenty
has poured her fruits upon Italy from brimming horn.

Horace's *Epistles* explicitly equate themselves with the *sermo*,
'conversation', of the *Satires*, but a letter bears an interesting
relation to face-to-face conversation. It is a surrogate
conversation, a substitute for the conversation you cannot have
because you are not in the same place as the recipient. As
Porphyrio, an ancient commentator on Horace, put it (at *Satires*
1.1), 'In his books of *Sermones* he wants it understood that he is
talking with someone present, as it were, while *Epistles* are sent to
people who are absent'. A letter, then, is a more formal kind of
conversation, the product of consideration, better organized, yet
still retaining certain characteristics of direct communication. It is
also only half of the conversation in an obvious sense, but a letter

makes efforts also to anticipate the response of the recipient. An ancient ideal of letter writing was that it should convey the whole person of the writer, and that is clearly an aim of Horace's collection. One is with Horace's *Epistles* once again encouraged to visualize the poet at a significant stage of life, now the mature, contemplative gentleman whose 'age is not what it was, nor his mentality' (1.1.4), and who can state as a principle, *non pudet lusisse, sed non incidere lusum*, 'It is no shame to have played around, but shameful not to curtail it' (1.14.36). But he also allows the character and circumstances of his addressees to shape his letters, again as a letter naturally would: in the fifth *Epistle*, for instance, Horace phrases his invitation to the barrister Torquatus in appropriately legalistic terms.

Less obviously, Horace captures with astonishing precision in the style of these poems the subtle distinctions that exist between epistolary and face-to-face interaction. The language is slightly less everyday than the *Satires*, and there is no obscenity (Horace in the *Epistles* is effectively sexless, amorous interest either far in the past or strictly hypothetical). There is more respect for the verse unit, and less messy collision between vowels. Yet though more respectable in these respects than satire, the *Epistles* avoid being positively poetic in their style—a realization in poetic form of the intermediate form of the letter, written but not literary. The expression and organization of these poems are also clearer than in the *Satires*, again reflecting the more measured character of something written as compared with the spontaneity of speech. Overall the book of *Epistles* presents itself as a more respectable exercise than satire. The twenty poems that comprise the first book amount to a tidy round number, and in the final poem Horace's book is a smart publication, 'polished with the pumice of the Sosii' (20.2), booksellers in Rome, as it heads out to its readership. But Horace also characterizes it as a runaway slave who will turn to prostitution, and imagines its unglamorous future teaching schoolchildren their ABC, so the insistence on the low aspirations of this conversational poetry persists, whether spoken or written.

Above all, perhaps, as conversation, albeit the more formal kind conducted through letters, the *Epistles* maintain, indeed intensify, Horace's persistent concern with friendship, *amicitia*. A letter is stereotypically addressed to a friend, and Horace's letters differ from satire again in offering guidance rather than criticism (albeit the criticism in Horace's satire was rarely especially harsh or directed), the hard-won insights of an older man. A medieval definition of the difference between Horace's satire and his epistolary verse is more right than wrong: 'following the method of a good farmer, he sowed the virtues [in the *Epistles*] where he had rooted out the vices [in the *Satires*]' (*Sciendum Commentary, Accessus* 1.6–7).

Epistle 1.3 can illustrate how Horace creates the impression of a communication from a concerned older friend. It is addressed to Iulius Florus, who was serving on the staff of Tiberius, the future emperor (a presence here as in the fourth book of *Odes*), in a campaign to establish a friendly king on the throne of Armenia, a country strategically placed between the Roman Empire and the Parthian Empire to the east. Horace enquires where Florus currently is, and what the other members of Tiberius' staff were up to—specifically, what poetry each is writing. A position on a general's staff was an established step on the career ladder for elite young men, and their role might be as much as anything to provide the senior man with stimulating company. Horace offers some amiable guidance that extends beyond poetry, encouraging Florus himself to find ways to control the anxieties attendant upon a young man's ambitions.

But at the end of the poem Horace turns to what, it is implied, is his real reason for writing, Florus' regrettable estrangement from a mutual friend (1.3.30–6), and the impression is effectively conveyed of a letter sent on a pretext:

> This too you must tell me when you reply, whether you covet
> Munatius as much as you should. Or is your friendship, poorly
> stitched up, failing to heal and tearing apart again? But whether

hot blood or inexperience of the world provokes you
wild young men with your untamed necks, wherever on earth
you are—too good as you are to break the bond of brotherhood—
there is a heifer I have vowed in anticipation of the return of
    you both.

Horace's poetry reconciles the two young men in its own fashion.

Roman friendship was at times closer to what we might call
networking, the cultivation of useful contacts. So when Horace
offers guidance to young ambitious men on how best to court
powerful men who could advance their careers, as he does in
Epistle 17 and at greater length in 18, this also, to Roman thinking,
is to tackle the topic of friendship as a key element of social life. At
issue in the latter poem is the distinction in Rome, intolerably fuzzy
but all the more critical for that, between a mercenary hanger-on
(a *scurra* or *parasitus*) and a true gentlemanly friend. Horace is
thus showing young men how to advance in Rome as the first book
of *Satires* had recounted Horace himself doing. But his own
relations with his more powerful friend, Maecenas, are directly at
issue in 7, where he justifies to his patron his prolonged absence
from Rome. In such places the perennial issue of *libertas* again
asserts itself, the key principle of Roman selfhood that here, as in
the *Satires*, Horace increasingly treats as a matter of private
relations between friends, or indeed between a man and his own
impulses. *Epistles* 1.7 has been an important point of reference for
more recent authors who saw in Horace's relationship with
Maecenas an ideal balance of autonomy and support, although
they have tended to define that balance as it suited their own
circumstances.

The letter to Aristius Fuscus, 1.10, of which we have already seen
the sign-off from the shrine of Vacuna, offers an image of
friendship that is more congenial to modern tastes, and also,
situated as it is in the centre of the collection, represents for
Horace himself something of an ideal. Fuscus features elsewhere

in Horace's poetry, mischievously refusing to rescue him from his bothersome companion in *Satires* 1.9, for instance, and one thing that can be concluded is that Aristius Fuscus had a healthy sense of humour; another, although it requires a little more effort to see it, is that he was a Stoic, a follower of the philosophical school that was often considered the chief rival of Epicureanism, with which Horace, albeit undogmatically, tended to associate himself.

A rough summary of 1.10 would be that Horace constructs a Stoic case for the Epicurean ideal of retirement from the stress of public life, but that doesn't capture the charm of this sparring between firm friends, one of whom, Fuscus, prefers the city, and the other the country, but never to the point of imperilling their fondness for each other (1.10.20–5):

> Is the water purer that strains to burst the pipes in the streets
> than what purls and murmurs down the sloping stream?
> Clearly it is, since trees grow among your mottled columns,
> and that house is preferred which boasts a view of distant fields.
> Turf Nature out with a pitchfork, but back she'll always rush
> and burst stealthily through all your ill-gotten distaste, triumphant.

A motto there for all half-hearted gardeners: any victory against Nature is strictly temporary, so why bother?

A joy for readers of Horace's Latin, and the despair of translators, is his gift for the memorable turn of phrase, as much in evidence in the *Epistles* as in the *Odes. Caelum non animum mutant qui trans mare currunt*, he warns the globetrotting Bullatius, 'They change the sky, not their state of mind, who rush across the sea' (1.11.27; John Milton could quote this to convey that he had ventured to Catholic Italy without losing his Protestant integrity; it is the epigraph also of David Lodge's campus novel *Changing Places*); while to Scaeva he proffers *sedit qui timuit ne non succederet*, 'He who feared he might not win stayed seated' (17.37); and to Lollius, *nam tua res agitur, paries cum proximus ardet, | et neglecta solent incendia sumere uires,* 'For it's your concern too when the neighbour's walls on fire, | and fires unaddressed have a habit of running riot' (1.18.84–5). But these aphorisms were not coined for their own sake. 'Whatever advice you give, make it short, so that what is quickly said | minds may readily grasp and faithfully retain', advises Horace in the *Ars Poetica* (335–6). The paedagogical claims of this poetry are sincere, and memorable tags an excellent way of making philosophy stick in the readers' minds. Greco-Roman philosophy, fundamentally concerned as it was with human life and how best to live it, was expert also in how to guide and persuade. The adage, like the power of the letter as a vehicle of guidance, was something that Horace learned from the philosophical tradition. He also understood that a message of self-improvement was more palatable when it came from someone with his own flaws, and Horace never comes across as anything but a human addressing other humans. Epistle 1.15, in which Horace admits to a weakness for a pampered life in a seaside resort, typically subverts the message of 1.14, in which Horace pokes fun at the *uilicus*, bailiff, of his country estate, who yearns for the fleshpots of Rome. In the later poem he compares himself to a character in Lucilius' satires, Maenius, who boasted of the simplicity of his lifestyle when times were hard, but was happy also to indulge himself when the opportunity arose, and the effect is similar to *Satires* 2.7 after 2.6, Horace puncturing his own complacent self-image.

An example of a more sober piece of philosophical guidance than his letter to Fuscus (with a reminder that the tone of these letters mimics the variety of any authentic correspondence) is 1.16, a powerful promotion of true, as opposed to pretended, virtue. Addressed to Quinctius, it opens with a charming description of Horace's estate in the Sabine country (Figure 7). But then the poem turns to Quinctius, and to ethical matters: *tu recte uiuis, si curas esse quod audis,* 'You live the good life, if you take care to *be* what people say you are' (1.16.17). Quinctius, Horace fears, is mistaking appearances for reality, praise for true virtue, and the

7. 'View of Horace's Villa' by Jacob More (1740–93), a Scottish landscape painter resident in Italy.

poem moves from that opening vignette of the carefree countryside to high seriousness, coloured with the austerity of Stoic ethics. It ends with a paraphrase of a scene from a tragic drama. King Pentheus is threatening the priest of Dionysus, whom he has in custody, but the priest refuses to be browbeaten (1.16.73–9):

> The good and wise man will have the courage to say, 'Pentheus,
> ruler of Thebes, what indignity will you force me
> to endure?' 'I'll take away your possessions.' 'Herds, property,
> fine furnishings, silverware, you mean? Take them.' 'I shall keep you
> in handcuffs and leg irons in the control of a brutal gaoler.'
> 'The god himself, whenever I wish it, will set me free.' I think
> this means, 'I shall die'. Death is the finishing line for everything.

Death, the inevitable end for everyone, can provide the perspective from which Quinctius should be able to discern a life of mere appearances from one that is truly well lived.

A letter to another young acquaintance (like Florus serving with Tiberius), 1.8, is short enough to be quoted in its entirety, and illustrates many of the characteristics of the collection:

To Celsus Albinovanus bear greetings and good wishes,
Muse, at my request, the companion and secretary of Nero.
If he asks how I am, tell him that, though promising many
    fine things,
my life is neither good nor pleasant. Not because hail
has flattened my vines and heat gnawed at my olives,
nor because my herd is sickening in distant pastures,
but because, healthy in body but less so in mind,
I won't listen to anything, or learn anything, to relieve my sickness,
I quarrel with well-meaning doctors, and I get angry with friends
when they try to rescue me from this fatal listlessness;
because I choose what does me harm, avoid what I think will
    help me,
love Tivoli when I'm in Rome, Rome when in Tivoli, as flighty as
    a breeze.
Next ask after *his* health, how he's faring, how he conducts himself,
how he is getting on with the prince and his staff.
If he says, 'Well', first be sure to express your delight, then
    straight after
to drip this piece of advice in the dear chap's ears:
'As you bear your good fortune, so will we, Celsus, bear you.'

The letter starts with epistolary greetings, elegantly varied, and in fact the poem plays throughout with the literal meaning of these formulae that wish good health and success. Horace then shares his own malaise, so deep that even his clear preference in the *Epistles* for life away from Rome's urban bustle is less certain. But this self-exposure is tactical, illustrating to his young friend that self-criticism is healthy, but also softening the firm advice he goes on to offer Celsus (who also, of course, receives the honour of a visit from Horace's Muse) not to take his success for granted. Celsus' name, which means 'lofty' or 'proud', is given an unusual emphasis at the end of the poem, and that is because its self-important owner could do with being taken down a peg or two, in the kindest, most diplomatic way.

The first book of *Epistles* is a carefully shaped poetic book. The second book of Horace's *Epistles* is more mysterious in its timing and genesis. It contains two poems, one (2.1) addressed to the Emperor Augustus and the other (2.2) to Iulius Florus (as *Epistles* 1.3 had been), and they are much longer than the poems of the first book. We have in addition Horace's longest, most influential, and most difficult poem, the *Ars Poetica*. A reasonable guess is that the two poems of the second book were originally independent compositions that were combined into a book after Horace's death, and some attempts to date them place 2.2 (to Florus) close in time to the first book, and 2.1, which alludes to the *Carmen Saeculare* in 17 BCE, a few years later. Plenty would disagree, however, and place both poems late in Horace's life. Meanwhile the *Ars Poetica* defeats even that level of speculation, its date a complete mystery, though many scholars think it is one of Horace's last compositions.

We can say a little more about the character of these poems. At the end of his poem to Augustus he describes what he is writing as *sermones … | … repentis per humum*, 'conversations that crawl along the ground' (2.1.250–1), much as he insists that he'd like to compose for the emperor grand flights of epic poetry on the conquests with which he had brought universal peace. In the *Ars Poetica*, similarly, Horace insists as he offers extensive direction on writing that he is 'writing nothing himself' (*Ars Poetica* 306). The short ancient biography of Horace, the core of which we can trace back to Suetonius, who had access to imperial archives, records a complaint from Augustus, after reading Horace's 'Conversations' (his satires or *Epistles*), that 'in your numerous writings of this kind you do not speak with me rather than everyone else', and that this provoked his poem to Augustus. This is as may be, but we recognize at least the emperor's characterization of this style of poetry as a conversation between poet and addressee. In fact both this poem and the *Ars Poetica* resemble Horace's satires in their loose structure, and unlike the poem to Florus make no explicit claim to be letters.

The poem to Augustus begins with praise of Horace's addressee.
The Roman People give Augustus the respect while alive that is
generally accorded great men only when they've died, he says.
But in poetry the Romans display less discretion, irrationally
preferring the long-dead to the poetry written by Horace and his
contemporaries. In discursive fashion, he describes and compares
the histories of Greek and Roman literature, emphasizing the
profound influence of the former on the latter, in the process
chiding the Romans for their attachment to archaic and
unsophisticated literature, the early poetry of Naevius and Ennius
and literature of the theatre especially, and neglect of the recent
achievements of such poets as Virgil and Varius. Augustus' taste in
poetry is by contrast impeccable, as his encouragement of those
poets proves, and Horace's conclusion is typically satirical, a denial
of his own ability to write a Virgilian epic of praise for Augustus
(while effectively doing so for six lines or so), and a prediction of
the fate of bad poetry, used for wrapping goods in the shopping
district. Much attention has been given to how Horace speaks
when addressing Augustus at such length, and modern critics
have found in the conclusion of the poem the tension between
poetic independence and patronage at its tautest. But it might be
countered that here as in *Odes* 4.15 respect is expressed within the
recognized conventions of the poetic genres he has adopted.

A striking moment in this poem sees Horace reminding Augustus,
as well as the general reader, of the poet's most public
achievement, his *Carmen Saeculare*. His point at this juncture is
the social value of the poet (2.1.132–8). 'From whom would the
girl, unknown to a husband, along with faultless boys, | learn her
prayers', Horace asks,

> if the Muse had not given her a bard?
> Their chorus seeks help and feels the presence of the gods,
> requests waters from heaven, persuasive with the prayer he
>   has taught,
> turns aside diseases, drives away dreadful dangers,

secures peace and a year rich in harvests.
With poetry the gods above are appeased, with poetry the
    gods below.

Epistle 2.2, the letter to Florus, is only superficially about
literature, and is in fact a superbly paced restatement of his
insistence in the first book of *Epistles* that philosophy is the
only worthwhile activity. Florus, Horace says, has requested a
letter and lyric poetry from him (gestures towards a larger
correspondence are another way of mimicking reality), and he
responds with a series of excuses for his failure to comply, none
of them entirely serious: Florus knew already what a poor
correspondent Horace was; Horace now lacked the drive to
write that he had had when impoverished after Philippi; people
couldn't decide what kind of poetry he should write; Rome was
an impossible place if you needed to concentrate, and so on.
But then comes the final excuse (2.2.141–4):

> The truth is that it is beneficial to throw away toys and learn wisdom,
> to leave to children the play that suits their age,
> and not search out words fit for setting to the Latin lyre
> but master the rhythms and measures of real life.

Could more powerful words come from the author of the *Odes*?
The tone becomes more sombre, and it is all the more compelling
for the light touch thus far. Horace pillories the claim of wealth to
provide satisfaction, then broadens the ethical exhortation with a
resounding coda (2.2.210–16):

> Are you grateful when you count up your birthdays? Are you
>   forgiving of your friends?
> Are you growing gentler and better as old age approaches?
> What good does it do you to extract just one thorn out of many?
> If you do not know how to live well, make way for those who do.
> You have played enough, you have eaten and drunk enough.

It's time for you to leave, lest, when you've drunk more than
   you should,
a generation more fittingly frivolous laugh at you and push you out.

Horace's letter to Florus provided inspiration for Juvenal in his
satire on the city of Rome, itself a highly influential text, and was
imitated directly by Alexander Pope in *The Second Epistle of the
Second Book of Horace*. It is the ultimate expression of Horace's
epistolary turn, congenial but sincere, to philosophy.

In the medieval manuscripts that preserved Horace's poetry, the
Ars Poetica stood as an independent work, and although it is
another hexametrical *sermo*, it stands apart in other respects as
well. The title we know it by was current as early as Quintilian, a
century after Horace, but is misleading, *ars* strongly suggesting a
technical treatise when it is really no such thing. (Quintilian at
least seems to confirm that this poem was a book on its own, a
self-standing composition separate from any other.) The poem
does indeed discuss poetic composition, with particular reference
to drama, and the nature of the poet's calling, with emphasis on
decorum or appropriateness, but it does so in a way that has
frustrated attempts to identify a coherent argument, or any
guidance that is particularly germane to a poet of Horace's time.
'This problematic work will seem different to one person than
another, and different again to each of them every ten years',
commented Goethe (*Annalen* 1806), speaking for many of us. But
if assessed by content and purpose it can seem baffling and jejune,
in expression the *Ars Poetica* is consummate, as anyone who has
talked of a *laudator temporis acti*, purple patches, or texts that
launch themselves *in medias res* tacitly acknowledges.

Here is Horace brilliantly contrasting the unimaginative opening
of an inferior epic poem by a so-called 'Cyclic poet' with Homer's
incomparable narrative gift, illustrated by the beginning of the
Odyssey (*Ars Poetica* 136–45):

Nor are you to begin like the Cyclic writer once did:
'Of Priam's fate and the famous war I shall sing.'
What will he produce worthy of that portentous opening?
The mountains will labour and what will be born? A silly little mouse.
How much better is Homer, whose efforts never end in foolishness:
'Tell me of the man, Muse, who after the capture of Troy
saw the ways of life of many men, and their cities.'
He aims to give, not smoke after fire, but after smoke
light, so that then he can bring out pleasing marvels
like Antiphates and Scylla and Charybdis and the Cyclops.

One thing Horace certainly doesn't do in the *Ars Poetica* is observe his own prescriptions. A poem must be *simplex et unus*, for instance, 'a single, homogeneous whole' (23), which the *Ars* itself is notoriously not, and it must use an appropriate metre: the *Ars Poetica* is written in a metre, the dactylic hexameter, that the *Ars* insists is the proper vehicle for 'the achievements of kings and generals and grim warfare'—epic poetry, in other words. But then the *Ars* claims, like all Horace's 'conversational' poetry, that it isn't poetry at all, and there is much to be said for the critic Niall Rudd's suggestion that, far from being any kind of 'systematic handbook of literary theory', the *Ars Poetica* is 'a lively, entertaining, verse-epistle, written by a well-read man for his friends, who shared his love of poetry and whose company we are invited to join'. If so, many of Horace's subsequent readers have gloriously misjudged it.

A final word on Horace's friends, though. The *Ars Poetica* is addressed to a father and two sons named Piso (an alternative modern name for the poem is the *Epistle to the Pisones*), and the likeliest identification of the father is a prominent figure in Roman public life under Augustus and Tiberius called L. Calpurnius Piso, who had proven literary interests: a Greek poet, Antipater of Thessalonica, in a poem some degrees more straightforward than the *Ars Poetica*, offers Piso a *kausia*, the Macedonian national hat, as a gesture of thanks for his defence of

Macedonia (*Anthologia Palatina* 6.335). If one of those sons had ambitions to write drama, that might make more sense of Horace's emphases. There are interesting connections also between an Epicurean philosopher and poet based on the Bay of Naples called Philodemus, a companion of Piso's father, and associates of Horace. In fragments of Philodemus' philosophy extracted from the Villa of the Papyri at Herculaneum (where a number of ancient bookrolls, carbonized by the action of Vesuvius in 79 CE, have survived), and painstakingly deciphered, Philodemus addresses Virgil, Varius, Plotius, and Quintilius. The first three of these are named as Horace's friends and literary confidants in *Satires* 1.5 and 1.10, while Quintilius' style as an editor is celebrated in an affectionate pen sketch in the *Ars Poetica* (438–44):

> If you ever read anything to Quintilius, 'Please change
> X and Y,' he would say. If you said you couldn't do better
> after two or three vain attempts, he'd tell you to scratch it out
> and return the badly turned verses to the anvil.
> If you chose to defend your offence rather than correct it,
> He wouldn't expend a single word further or waste any effort
> to stop you loving yourself and your work alone and without a rival.

Quintilius' death had been marked in one of the *Odes* (1.24), a poem addressed to Virgil in which Horace toyed with the idea of death as something unsusceptible to any kind of editing or rewriting. In the *Ars Poetica*, then, which *may* be Horace's last poem, there is just a glimpse also of the intellectual company that Horace kept and that shaped Horace as a poet.

Chapter 6
Horace after Horace

In the last poem of his three-book *Odes* collection, Horace had expressed the confident hope, *non omnis moriar, multaque pars mei | uitabit Libitinam: usque ego postera | crescam laude recens, dum Capitolium | scandet cum tacita uirgine pontifex*, 'I shall not entirely die, and a greater part of me will escape the goddess of funerals. In time to come I shall keep on growing, my fame ever fresh, so long as the Chief Priest climbs the Capitol alongside the silent Vestal Virgin' (3.30.6–9). Horace aspired to be read as long as Rome was Rome, and has in fact outlasted the Roman state rituals that seemed to him the ultimate yardstick of permanence. (Horace places the word *tacita*, 'silent', evoking the meticulous religious observance of the Vestal Virgil, just before a pause, a silence, in the verse: it is a vivid pen sketch.) The future envisaged at the end of his first book of *Epistles* is less glamorous—popular initially, but then abandoned to bookworms or the second-hand book trade, and finally serving as an aid for children learning their letters (1.20.9–18). Horace was indeed a school text through antiquity, and again, after a gap, from the 10th century; and in the new 'public' schools of the 19th century: in a 1st-century CE papyrus from Egypt a line of the *Ars Poetica* is set as a writing exercise.

The reception of any author is a matter of selection, certain favoured works typically treated as representative. But perhaps the most persistent feature of Horace's afterlife was the conviction that in Horace's poetry one was encountering a recognizable individual, the dependable friend or travelling companion described by Coleridge as 'the man whose works have been in all ages deemed the models of good sense, and are still the pocket companions of those who pride themselves on uniting the scholar with the gentleman'. James Joyce, similarly, talks of the 'human pages' of Stephen Dedalus' 'timeworn Horace' that 'never felt cold to the touch even when his own fingers were cold'. It tended to be something more than imitation, the relationship with Horace: a proliferation of latter-day 'Horaces' across Europe (the 'Polish Horace', Maciej Kazimierz Sarbiewski, a Latin poet in the 17th century, was particularly renowned), identified by themselves or their readers in a way we do not find with Virgil or Ovid, suggests its intensity. We began this book, of course, with Aurel Stein finding comfort in another well-fingered copy of Horace's works. So maybe in the *Epistles* he was half-right. But this idealized image of Horace as an archetypal gentleman, in the 18th and 19th centuries especially (although already in the Middle Ages, Horace's works were felt to represent a model of a human life), inevitably shaped which poems were preferred for reading or imitation.

The *Epodes*, for instance, some of which conflicted sharply with Horace's image as the mature and genial dispenser of wisdom, feature less than his other works, and *Epodes* 8 and 12, with their explicit content, were left out of even academic publications, along with comparably obscene sections of *Satires* 1.2. But an illustrative exception in the *Epodes* is the second epode, which perhaps counts as the most translated poem in Horace's whole oeuvre, but has rarely been translated in its entirety. *Epode* 2 is an extended evocation of an idealized rustic life, punctured in the last four lines by the revelation that the speaker is a daydreaming moneylender called Alfius with no intention of relocating to the countryside, and the tradition, almost universally (and beginning with the epigrammatist Martial, just a century after Horace), excised the uncomfortable coda to leave an untarnished rural idyll. Thomas Jefferson had lines from the poem inscribed on a fountain at Monticello, the slave-worked plantation in rural Virginia that he conceived as his retreat from the pressures of political life. A more subtle response could play the selectivity of the tradition against Horace's original. Victoria Moul has explained how a seemingly celebratory account by Ben Jonson of Sir Robert Wroth's life in the countryside (*Forest* 3), based on *Epode* 2, hints at the financial concerns of Horace's coda, and through them at the ruinous debts that Wroth's country estate had incurred. Jonson played a key role in the naturalization of classical models in English poetry, and his relationship with Horace was unusually intense, his claims to be a latter-day Horace echoed by his admirers. In his play *Poetaster* (1601), a defence of Jonson's satire against the attacks of John Marston and Thomas Dekker, the character of Horace, a figure of humble birth but high moral integrity, clearly reflects Jonson himself, and central to the plot of the play is a staging of Horace's uncomfortable stroll through Rome in *Satires* 1.9.

Even in the *Odes* the affection expressed for adolescents like Ligurinus in the fourth book, a central feature of the lyric tradition, was also reliably bowdlerized. But in more general terms also, of the 103 poems certain examples were especially favoured. Ronald Storrs, a colonial administrator whom T. E. Lawrence called 'the most brilliant Englishman in the Near East', collected hundreds of versions of *Odes* 1.5, the so-called 'Pyrrha Ode'. After his death, sixty-three English versions and eighty-one in a range of other languages were published in *Ad Pyrrham* (1959). Part of the reason for this poem's popularity is that it exemplifies Horace's radical experiments with word combination, and is thus a particular challenge to translate (the difficulty of translating him, far from deterring, encouraged translators, of course): John Milton attempted a 'metaphrase' (copying the original metre, and as closely as possible the Latin word order) which divides opinion, but certainly makes of Pyrrha, 'plain in thy neatness', a more puritanical young woman than the manslayer that Horace had in mind.

Odes 1.22 was another popular poem, but a fascinating aspect of its afterlife illustrates the ever presence of editing. It opens on a philosophical note, suggesting Stoic ideals of enlightened impassivity (1–8):

> The man pure in life and innocent of crime
> needs not Mauretanian javelins nor bow
> nor quiver swollen with poison-tipped
> arrows, Fuscus,
>
> whether he is setting out across the broiling
> Syrtes, or the unwelcoming
> Caucasus, or the places lapped
> by the storied Jhelum.

The involvement of Aristius Fuscus, elsewhere associated both with Stoicism and with facetious behaviour, hints that something else is going on here, and indeed, after providing evidence of his philosophical invulnerability (a wolf in the Sabine country that spontaneously ran away from him), Horace attributes his security not to Stoic wisdom, but to the lover, Lalage, about whom he'd been singing when he encountered the animal. In the 19th century the first or first two stanzas of the poem, their flippant continuation suppressed, were given a sombre musical setting by F. F. Flemming and became a hymn standard at north-European funerals. Jesuit school texts, meanwhile, jesuitically replaced Lalage's name with *socios*, '[male] comrades'. Fuscus would have found both circumstances most amusing.

There have been regular efforts to set the self-proclaimed 'songs' of the *Odes* to music, all of which inevitably struggle, not only with the verbal and thematic complexity of Horace's lyric, but also with abbreviated and repeated stanzaic forms, which do not readily suit modern musical styles. But settings by Orlando de Lassus of *Epode* 2 and Cipriano de Rore of *Odes* 3.9 in the 16th century are intriguing, in each case adopting the motet form proper to sacred scripture, an indication of the prestige of Horace's text. Lassus misses out the jaundiced coda of the epode, needless to say, while Rore's setting of an exchange between estranged lovers in 3.9 gives the woman's stanzas to female singers and the man's to male, but concludes with a glorious polyphonic setting of the final stanza as the lovers are reconciled. The *Carmen Saeculare*, Horace's only composition that was written to be sung, found a disturbingly congenial new life, with its interest in purity and *Romanità*, in 1930s Italy, where the chorus of Gian Francesco Malipiero's opera *Giulio Cesare* sang stanzas from the *Carmen* during a concluding scene when Caesarian forces fresh from victory at Philippi occupy the stage. The Arch of the Philaeni (Figure 8), an Italian Fascist monument which stood on the main road along the coast in Libya, marking the boundary between the Italian colonial possessions of Tripolitania and Cyrenaica, bore in huge letters the same text from the *Carmen* that Malipiero's chorus opened with, which had become practically a Fascist motto: 'Life-giving Sun, may you look upon nothing greater than the city of Rome'. The arch was demolished by Colonel Gadaffi in 1973.

8. The Arch of the Philaeni, an Italian Fascist monument that stood until 1973 on the coast road in northern Libya, and carried words from the *Carmen Saeculare*.

In antiquity itself, Horace's posthumous influence can at first sight appear limited. There was no vibrant tradition of Latin lyric poetry kick-started by his *Odes*, for instance, nor of philosophical verse letters—before the Renaissance at least. In iambic verse, as it persists in Martial's epigrams at the end of the 1st century CE, Catullus is a more obvious influence than Horace. The tradition of satire begun by Lucilius was picked up after Horace by Persius, in whose crabbed and vivid verse it has been said that barely a line is free of Horatian language, and in Juvenal, who reverts to a more aggressive style superficially closer to Lucilius'.

But if the remarkable innovations of *numerosus Horatius* ('many-metred Horace', the description of his younger contemporary, Ovid, *Tristia* 4.10.49) discouraged direct imitation, his presence in later authors is obvious enough. One illustration might be the fourth book of the *Silvae* of P. Papinius Statius, dating to 95 CE, a collection of occasional poems addressed to the Emperor Domitian along with a collection of elite Romans. Poem 4.4, to Vitorius Marcellus, is an epistle from Statius in Naples to Marcellus in Rome that closely imitates Horace's letters in its informal style, its attention to the circumstances of writer and recipient, a younger man, and its interest in themes such as friendship and relaxation; Statius locates himself as he writes by the tomb of Virgil, still today pointed out in Naples, as Horace had placed himself by the temple of Vacuna. But the following three poems also evoke Horace, 4.5 and 4.7 adopting the alcaic and sapphic metres that he favoured in the *Odes*, and imitating the style and moral and literary themes of Horace's lyrics. Meanwhile the sixth poem works round to describing a miniature statue of Hercules that had supposedly once belonged to Alexander the Great, Hannibal, and the Roman dictator Sulla, but opens with a passage imitating the conversational style of Horace's satires, and a scene (Statius strolling aimlessly through the centre of Rome) lifted from Horace's *Satires* 1.9.

If we ask why Statius emphasized his debt to Horace in these poems, imitation of this kind was its own justification for Roman poets, as we have seen, a way of asserting one's own claim to comparable poetic status: Catullus and Virgil are also important models for Statius in this book. But the Horatian atmosphere that Statius carefully constructs also supports the poet's characterization of himself in this book as a man embracing some form of retreat from Rome to the more congenial environment of the Bay of Naples. What Horace represented more than anything for posterity was someone who knew how to retire in an intellectually constructive way. David Hume, having accepted in his early 50s a diplomatic posting to Paris in 1763, took just four books with him, Virgil, Horace, Tasso, and Tacitus, but of Horace he remarked, 'I own that in common decency, I ought to have left my *Horace* behind me, and that I ought to be ashamed to look him in the face. For I am sensible that at my years no temptation would have seduced *him* from his retreat.'

Prudentius, at the beginning of the 5th century, is considered the first great Christian poet, and offers another parallel, prefacing a collection of his religious poetry with a poem that echoes the first poems of *Odes* 4 and *Epistles* 1 to explain his determination, at the age of 57, to apply himself to more serious tasks in the twilight of his days. Metrical forms reminiscent of Horace's in his lyrics carry Prudentius' renewed commitment to 'sing of the Lord, | fight against heresies, disseminate the Catholic | faith, trample down the rites of the heathen, | visit ruin upon your idols, Rome, | dedicate song to the martyrs, and exalt the apostles' (*Praefatio* 38–42). An answer of sorts to St Jerome's pressing question on the Christian value of pagan literature, 'What has Horace to do with the Psalter?' (*Epistulae* 22.29). A more comprehensive answer is provided by George Buchanan, tutor to both Mary Queen of Scots and her son James VI/I, and a celebrated Latin poet best known for his *Poetic Paraphrase of the Psalms of David* in Horace's or at least Horatian metres, 'seeking to clothe the poetic centrepiece of the Bible in contemporary and fashionable humanistic dress' (Stephen Harrison). Psalm 23, 'The Lord is my shepherd', is rendered in the same metre as Horace's poem for Agrippa (p. 10) and with language recognizably Horatian.

But as a poet imagined above all as existing in contemplative retreat, Horace exerted a particular influence on the 18th century. His villa in the Sabine hills struck a chord in a period that set special store by a 'villa ideal—in architectural terms that of actual houses built for rural . . . retreat, and ideological terms that of the pursuit . . . of a life of cultivated leisure, refined ease and intellectually profitable repose' (Iain Gordon Brown). Horace's descriptions of his estate (at the start of *Epistles* 1.16 especially), rather like his accounts of himself, were sufficiently short of specifics to encompass many permutations of this ideal. But an influential expression was the impressive Palladian villa and fine garden with classical trimmings constructed in the first half of the 18th century by Alexander Pope, an authority on horticulture as well as poetry, on the Thames at Twickenham, which at the time was comfortably outside London. In the cellars of his new house, and extending under an adjacent road and into his garden, Pope established a famous grotto, in which contemporary images depict him writing. At the garden entrance to this grotto (which is the only part of Pope's creation that still in part survives) was affixed a white marble plaque bearing the words from *Epistles* 1.18, SECRETUM ITER ET FALLENTIS SEMITA VITAE, 'a concealed journey and the byway of a life unseen' (*Epistles* 1.18.103), Horace's Epicurean prescription for the good life (Figure 9). Characteristically of Pope, the motto is apt both for an underpass into an unexpectedly charming garden and for a life of the mind pursued at a safe remove from the city.

Horace was as important to Pope as a poet as all this would suggest, and like his predecessor Ben Jonson, Pope's identification went deep. But his imitations of Horace maintain a dynamic relationship with the original, inspired by Horace at every stage, but freely adapting Horace's text to his own circumstances. Horace exemplified the polish and refinement that the 18th century, and Pope at its head, sought, and beyond that Pope, as a Catholic victim of officially sanctioned discrimination after William of Orange's seizure of power, found in his imitation of Horace an

9. 'View in Pope's Garden with His Shell Temple' by William Kent. Behind the 'Shell Temple' in the foreground can be seen the entrance to Pope's grotto, and over the door the stone that was inscribed with the text from the *Epistles*.

authoritative vehicle for self-expression as an independent man of letters. Here in *The Second Epistle of the Second Book of Horace Imitated* (1737) he offers his own version of Horace's description of his early deprivation and self-advancement through poetry (in Pope's case achieved through his successful translation of Homer's *Iliad*), though again presented as a reason not to write any more: John Monro was a physician at Bedlam. His heroic couplet, concise but clear, is a good match for Horace's epistolary hexameter at its most formal, and comparably quotable:

> But knottier points we knew not half so well,
> Deprived us soon of our paternal cell;
> And certain laws, by sufferers thought unjust,
> Denied all posts of profit or of trust:
> Hopes after hopes of pious Papists fail'd,
> While mighty William's thundering arm prevail'd.
> For right hereditary tax'd and fined,
> He stuck to poverty with peace of mind;
> And me, the Muses help'd to undergo it;
> Convict a Papist he, and I a poet.
> But (thanks to Homer) since I live and thrive,
> Indebted to no prince or peer alive,

Sure I would want the care of ten Monroes,
If I would scribble rather than repose.

Pope's quest for polite retirement is found also in John Toland's
Description of Epsom (1711), another exercise in celebrating the
delights of a retreat from London that enjoys a strong Horatian
colouring, seasoned also with some Pliny the Younger, another
owner of a life-restoring out-of-town villa: the title page bears the
motto *Quid quaeris? uiuo et regno*, from Horace's praise of his
country retreat in *Epistles* 1.10 to Fuscus, 'In a word, I live like a
king'. The intellectual element of this retreat could be associated
with other impulses of the Age of Reason. We have seen how the
Royal Society adapted a motto from Horace's statement of
philosophical independence to express its own commitment to
free thought, and Kant's claim for *sapere aude* as the slogan of the
Enlightenment. Diderot, in a seminal essay on Eclecticism in his
Encyclopédie, defined the ideal Enlightenment thinker, 'trampling
underfoot prejudice, tradition, ancientness, received wisdom,
authority, in a word everything that subjugates the mass of minds',
in relation to the same line as the Royal Society, *nullius addictus
iurare in uerba magistri*. In its origin, the independence that
Horace seeks in the *Epistles* is a delicate balance between
gratitude to Maecenas, whose generosity has made everything
possible, and his own private needs—no conflict at all, in reality.
But what tension there was allowed Ariosto in Horatian mode to
make a virtue of rejection by his patron, while Boileau could, with
equal justice, celebrate in Horace's terms the benefits of an
enlightened patron.

All this interest in Horace and villas drew attention to the
physical site of Horace's own villa, situated somewhere in the
Sabine hills. Horace left sufficient topographic clues to allow a not
especially impressive gathering of ruins to be identified near
Licenza, and it drew so many reverent English and Scottish
visitors that the locals came to believe that Horace had been an
Inglese. Giovanni Battista Piranesi, famous as he was for etchings

of eye-catching classical remains, satirized a three-volume contribution to the rediscovery of 'a dry spring and a few broken walls' with a map featuring 'Academy of the Fanatics', 'Corrupt Passages', 'Place Where the Authors Don't Agree', and at the centre a huge turd inscribed 'Ruins of Horace's Villa'. But 'our memory sees more than our eyes' at such sites, as Horace Walpole insisted.

But if Horace was an Englishman, he was also just as surely a German, a Frenchman, a Pole and a Hungarian, embodying a male elite ethos that was pan-European. Two Latin poems by the Spanish 16th-century poet and soldier Garcilaso de la Vega, imitating Horace in form and style, have recently been rediscovered by Maria Czepiel. They show Garcilaso, an exile from Spain, using Horace and the Latin language to forge and maintain relationships across Europe, in these two poems with the Venetian Pietro Bembo, scholar, poet, and future cardinal, and Johann Alexander Brassicanus, a German humanist favoured by the Holy Roman Emperor Maximilian I. Horace's model encouraged poets to write to each other about poetry, but was also a catalyst of friendship, here within the Renaissance Republic of Letters. A twenty-stanza Latin alcaic ode by Dr J. P. Steele published in *The Lancet* on 31 March 1894, in honour of Guido Baccelli, president of the Eleventh International Medical Congress in Rome, 1894, promoted the cohesion of a more modern sodality, and achieved a very fair imitation of his Horatian models. In a celebrated story, Patrick Leigh Fermor and Heinrich Kreipe, a British officer and his German captive on Crete in 1942, established a common understanding when Kreipe, gazing up at the peak of Mt Ida, quoted the opening of *Odes* 1.9, *uides ut alta stet niue candidum | Soracte*, 'You see how Mt Soracte stands bright white in deep snow', and Leigh Fermor continued the quotation to the end of the poem. 'We had both drunk at the same fountains long before', Leigh Fermor commented in *A Time of Gifts*, 'and things were different between us for the rest of our time together'. When he had walked across Europe in the 1930s, Leigh Fermor had carried

with him a Loeb parallel Latin/English text of the *Odes* and
Epodes like Aurel Stein's, and when he lost it he was gifted a
beautiful 17th-century text of the same poems by an aristocratic
German host. *A Time of Gifts* is haunted by the war to come, as
Horace's *Odes* had been by the war that had just passed. Nazi
educationalists tried hard to select odes for study in German
schools that reinforced their ideology, with some of the sentiments
of the 'Roman Odes' and *Carmen Saeculare* meeting their
requirements, but the essence of Horace's lyric, drinking and
friendship, was more apt for overcoming division. The rigidities of
20th-century militaristic ideologies in truth sat ill with it.

What the Leigh Fermor story also highlights is the memorability
of Horace's poetry. The artful word order of the *Odes*, especially,
has been the bugbear of generations of schoolchildren, but it is a
positive aid when one is piecing the jigsaw back together from
memory. 'Tout le monde aime Horace et le sait par coeur', stated
Gabriel-Henri Gaillard early in the 19th century. Leigh Fermor
recited poems of Horace as he tramped across Europe, alarming
the locals as he did so. Dr Johnson was in the habit of retreating to
a corner of the room and mumbling audibly as he recalled them,
perhaps countering the intense fear he harboured throughout his
life of losing his mind, as Richard Tarrant suggests. Whole poems
were one thing, but Horace is also eminently quotable in shorter
stretches. There are far more Horace quotations than any other
non-English source in the *Oxford Dictionary of Quotations*, and
whether in the pages of the *Idler* and *Tatler* in the 18th century or
Georgian and Victorian drawing rooms, or indeed in the House of
Commons, quoting Horace established one's education and status.
Often, as we have seen, those quotations found themselves visibly
engraved on something. According to J. M. Barrie's *Margaret
Ogilvy* (1896), his biography of his mother, a voracious reader
with little formal education but high ambitions for her children,
Margaret took great pleasure in peppering her conversation with
Horatian tags that she'd learned from her son, astounding the
'colleged men' she was addressing just so long as she could resist

bursting out laughing. Clubbable himself, Horace granted access to the club, on occasions quite literally: an application to join the Cotteswold Naturalists' Club in 1850 from W. Henry Hyett, former MP for Stroud, took the form of a witty parody of the 'Lalage Ode', *Odes* 1.22. Horace's Latin word *terminus*, 'boundary', is re-used to denote the new railway terminus at Gloucester, for instance.

Another Horatian motto, *Dulce et decorum est pro patria mori*, 'Sweet and honourable it is to die for one's country', has a certain notoriety since Wilfred Owen powerfully characterized it as 'the old Lie'. But before Owen's poem, it had graced the weathered and impossibly poignant memorial cross that now resides in the Chapel of the Durham Light Infantry in Durham Cathedral (Figure 10). The cross was erected on the summit of the Butte de Warlencourt immediately after the temporary capture of this elevated feature on the Somme battlefield in November 1916, and it stood there in all elements, wood imitating stone, until 1926, when it was placed in the cathedral. Dr Johnson, quoted by Boswell in his *Life of Johnson*, talked of the 'community of mind' that there was in the quotation and recognition of classical authors like Horace, and that isn't a negligible consideration.

Kipling said of his Latin teacher at school that '[W.C.] C[rofts] taught me to loathe Horace for two years; to forget him for twenty; and then to love him for the rest of my days and through many sleepless nights'. The idea of Horace as a poet for the middle aged, alert to their mortality, is a strong one, and answers to Horace's matching of genres to times of his own life. Translations of Horace tended to be an occupation for retirement, while W. H. Auden in *A Thanksgiving* naturally picks Horace as the ideal guide for his mellower years. Byron, Pound, and Brecht all came round to Horace only in later life, and to younger readers, absent the revelation of mortality and sense of proportion in things, he can easily seem too polished, lacking passion and sincerity, certainly not the poet for revolutionary fervour, even if Dryden's 'a temporizing poet, a well-mannered court slave'

10. Memorial cross in the Memorial Chapel of the Durham Light Infantry in Durham Cathedral. It was originally erected on the Butte de Warlencourt after its capture in November 1916 and bears the Horatian legend 'Sweet and honourable it is to die for one's country'.

overstates the case as Dryden was wont to do. A more subtle modern take on Horace's perceived complacency, middle class as well as middle aged, is Donald Davie's *Wombwell on Strike*, which addresses the 1984–5 Miners' Strike in stanzas reminiscent of Horace's, and, while disputing Dryden's characterization, compares his poetry to a train passing obliviously through a tunnel beneath the South Yorkshire Minefield where police and strikers fought, a cultivated voice inadequate to the crisis of the moment.

Kipling's engagement with Horace in later life was comparable in intensity to Jonson's and Pope's. A poem that accompanied his short story *Regulus*, which replayed the moral of one of Horace's 'Roman Odes' (3.5) in the lives of Kipling's erstwhile schoolmates, was a version of Horace's first ode reimagined in the context of a modern debate between Arts and Sciences. The poem is a brilliant pastiche, and inspired a peculiar project, *Q. Horati Flacci Carminum Liber Quintus* (1920), 'Horace's Odes Book 5'. In the event, Kipling's involvement was limited, only three of the fifteen poems translated into Horatian Latin by various classical hands being his compositions. A poem of Kipling that wasn't used—its rejection may have curtailed Kipling's involvement—imitates Horace in its clear but mannered word order, and captures one thing that Kipling found in Horace, which was a way of contemplating loss as a burden common to humanity. In *A Recantation (To Lyde of the Music Halls)* he addresses a popular entertainer to whom Kipling's son Jack, killed at Loos in 1915, had been devoted. Lyde is generally assumed to evoke the entertainer Harry Lauder, who had continued to perform in a comic revue entitled *Three Cheers* at the Shaftesbury after news had arrived of his own son's death in combat. Kipling and Lyde are united in the final stanza as word artists doing what they must do in spite of everything: 'Yet they who use the Word assigned | To hearten and make whole, | Not less than Gods have served mankind, | Though vultures rend their soul'. An altogether lighter exercise in Horatian imitation is Kipling's *Carmen*

Circulare, sage advice from the ancient poet on sensible motoring. Parody is perhaps the very best indication of wide currency.

From Kipling to the British Empire is not so great a leap, and the classically trained men who ruled India certainly brought Horace along with them. One consequence is a *ghazal* of the 17th-century Pashtun poet Khushal Khan Khattak translated by Sir Evelyn Howell, a senior civil servant in British India, into English and into Latin sapphic stanzas (appendix E in Olaf Caroe, *The Pathans*). Goethe had been reminded of Horace when reading the medieval Persian poet Hafez, and Persianate poems of love and wine with a strong emphasis on life's brevity were perhaps bound to put Europeans in mind of Horace: there is certainly a lot of Horace as well as Khayyam in Fitzgerald's *Rubaiyat*.

Correcting slightly the bias towards Horace's lyric poetry, Alistair Elliot's *On the Appian Way* (1984) is a book-length reenactment of Horace's travel poem, *Satires* 1.5, and at that length a fair impression of the significantly longer poem by Lucilius that Horace was himself imitating. We find the same unedifying details, matched by episodes of uneven and unpredictable length, colloquial diction, and disrespect for the poetic unit. Spotting the line of the ancient Appian Way, the satirist can't summon the energy to follow it: 'it's much less fuss | To barge across those marshes in a bus'. Ancient and modern transport across the Pomptine Marshes are nicely juxtaposed in 'barge…bus' (p. 12).

But the most influential of Horace's *sermones* by far has been the *Ars Poetica*. In the Renaissance the practical commonsense of the *Ars* was fused in imaginative ways with Aristotle's *Poetics*, a systematic account of poetry in a way that the *Ars* never was, and became by association an authoritative expression of classical literary principle. Translations of the *Ars* into the vernacular are closely associated with influential Renaissance literary movements like the Pléiade in France and Philip Sidney's Pembroke circle in England. The history of Horace's phrase *ut pictura poesis*, read in the Renaissance and beyond as an assertion of what poetry should aspire to be, and in turn shaping how different genres of paintings were valued and compared, and how the art of painting in general aspired to a seriousness equal to poetry—all at some significant remove from its point in Horace's text—is illustrative of the astonishing impact of this single poem. If poetry is like painting, Horace's advice on such things as the appropriate representation of various ages of human life in poetry could be applied to the art of painting at a formative moment in its development. The *Ars* had had a role in the later Middle Ages, too, but as a less exalted classroom guide to composition of Latin verse. In neither case, in truth, did it fit its new application very comfortably.

Locating women's voices in this tradition might appear comparably challenging, and there is no disputing the overwhelmingly masculine focus of Horace's poetry, an emphasis reflected in its reception. That said, Horace's poetry has not represented so uncongenial a subject for women as one might imagine. Aphra Behn and Lady Mary Montagu could both rewrite the 'Pyrrha Ode' with a male lothario as the central character, while more recently in 2002 a new version of the *Odes*, edited by J. D. McClatchy and by various hands, included an English *Fons Bandusiae* (*Odes* 3.13) by Eavan Boland. The unusual form adopted by Boland, six-line stanzas of iambic tetrameter, recalls, no doubt deliberately, a 17th-century version of the same ode, *To Mother Luddwels Cave and Spring*, by Martha, Lady Giffard: 'If I can give this fountain fame | It shall not want a Noble name | Nor will I fail the rock to sing | From whence thy murmuring waters spring | And the tall oaks that bending grow | And overshade its mossy Brow' (1–6).

The familiar Horatian stance of retirement to a private space might also suit the circumstances of an intelligent but socially restricted woman. One such was Elizabeth Tollett (1694–1754), who in *A Portrait* sketches her ideal life, including (23–30, with reference to the last line of *Odes* 4.12):

Friends that in any Dress would come;
To whom I'd always be at home:
My Table still shou'd cover'd be,
On this Side Books, on that Bohea;
While we sip on, and ne'er debate
Matters of Scandal, or of State.
For *Horace* tells us, as you know,
'Tis sweet to fool it *a propos*.

Bohea is tea, so it is a restrained kind of *symposium*.

A final devotee of Horace is Karl Heinrich Ulrichs, who in *Alaudae* ('Larks'), a Latin-language newspaper that he produced from L'Aquila in Italy between 1889 and 1895, wrote Latin poems in Horatian metres, discussed with a Finnish professor of Latin how appropriate Lalage's presence was at funerals, and adapted the ode about Mt Soracte to describe the mountain massif Gran Sasso that overlooks L'Aquila. A stated purpose of *Alaudae* was to promote the Latin language as a means of unifying the ominously divided Europe of the late 19th century—and *Alaudae* achieved an impressive circulation across the continent and beyond—but Ulrichs had come to L'Aquila after a life of courageous campaigning within Germany for the toleration of homosexuality, and elsewhere he takes William Gladstone to task for glossing over the homosexual material of book 4 in the translation of the *Odes*, largely composed on train journeys during general election campaigning, which he published in 1894 after resigning as prime minister. Horace finds a role in both of Ulrichs' projects, a voice that had become the common currency of educated Europe, but an authority also capable, by virtue of his origin in a culture quite unlike those that had adopted him, of unsettling established opinion and espousing causes revolutionary in their time.

Further reading

There are many translations available of the *Odes* and *Carmen Saeculare*, including James Michie (1967); David West (2008, the *Odes, Epodes* and *Carmen Saeculare*); Stephanie McCarter (2020); and N. Rudd translated the *Satires* and *Epistles* along with the Satires of Persius (2005). D. S. Carne-Ross and K. Haynes (eds.), *Horace in English* (1996) collects together English versions of all his works.

David West produced three excellent volumes on *Odes*, books 1–3, with Latin text, English translation, and an accessible discussion of each poem by one of the greatest recent Horatian scholars: *Horace, Odes I: Carpe Diem* (1995); *Horace, Odes II: Vatis Amici* (1999); *Horace, Odes III: Dulce Periculum* (2002). R. G. M. Nisbet and M. Hubbard published more detailed commentaries on *Odes* I (1970) and *Odes* II (1978), and R. G. M. Nisbet and N. Rudd on *Odes* III (2004).

Horace is also very well served by collections of essays that cover all his works and their reception after his death, on which this book has drawn extensively:

C. D. N. Costa (ed.), *Horace* (1973)
G. Davis (ed.), *A Companion to Horace* (2010)
K. Freudenburg (ed.), *Horace: Satires and Epistles* (2009)
B. D. Frischer and I. G. Brown (eds.), *Allan Ramsay and the Search for Horace's Villa* (2001)
H.-Chr. Günther (ed.), *Brill's Companion to Horace* (2013)
S. J. Harrison (ed.), *Homage to Horace* (1995)
S. J. Harrison (ed.), *The Cambridge Companion to Horace* (2007)

L. B. T. Houghton and M. Wyke (eds.), *Perceptions of Horace* (2009)

M. Lowrie (ed.), *Horace: Odes and Epodes* (2009)

C. Martindale (ed.), *Horace Made New* (1993)

N. Rudd (ed.), *Horace 2000, a Celebration* (1993)

Good introductions slightly longer than this one are P. Hills, *Horace* (2005) and R. Tarrant, *Horace's Odes* (2020), the latter of which covers his whole career by way of context for the *Odes*.

Aside from these works and those cited in the references, I have borrowed ideas from M. Czepiel, "Two Newly Discovered Poems by Garcilaso de la Vega", *Bulletin of Spanish Studies* 99 (2022), 741–776; D. C. Feeney, *Literature and Religion at Rome* (1998); E. Gowers, *The Loaded Table: Representations of Food in Roman Literature* (1993); P. R. Hardie, 'The Ars Poetica and the Poetics of Didactic', *Materiali e discussioni per l'analisi dei testi classici* 72 (2014), 43–54; S. J. Harrison, 'Fuscus the Stoic: Horace Odes 1.22 and Epistles 1.10', *The Classical Quarterly* 42 (1992), 543–47; and "George Buchanan: the Scottish Horace", in L.B.T. Houghton and G. Manuwald, *Neo-Latin Poetry in the British Isles* (2012), 155–72; N. McDowell, *Poet of Revolution: The Making of John Milton* (2020); myself, 'The One and Only Fons Bandusiae', *The Classical Quarterly* 59 (2009), 132–41 (which should be balanced by I.-K. Sir, 'Horace Odes 3.13: Intertexts and Interpretation', *The Classical Quarterly* (forthcoming)); V. Moul, *Jonson, Horace and the Classical Tradition* (2010); M. C. J. Putnam, *Horace's 'Carmen Saeculare': Ritual Magic and the Poet's Art* (2001); N. Rudd, *Horace: Epistles II and 'Ars Poetica'* (1989), 34; L. Rásonyi, *Stein Aurél és hagyatéka* (1960); R. J. Tarrant, '*Lyricus vates*: musical settings of Horace's *Odes*', *Yale Classical Studies* 36, 72–93; C. Whitton, 'Minerva on the Surrey Downs', *The Cambridge Classical Journal* 60 (2014), 127–57; A. B. Willson, 'Alexander Pope's Grotto in Twickenham', *Garden History* 26 (1998), 31–59; and Th. Ziolkowski, 'Uses and Abuses of Horace: His Reception Since 1935 in Germany and Anglo-America', *International Journal of the Classical Tradition* 12 (2005–6), 183–215.

I also offer the following list of non-classical sources: M. A. Stein, *Sand-buried ruins of Khotan* (1903), 235; J. Joyce, *A Portrait of the Artist as a Young Man* (1916), 209; E. Kant, "Beantwortung der Frage: Was ist Aufklärung?", *Berlinische Monatsschrift* 4 (1784), 481–94; R. Kipling, *A Diversity of Creatures* (1917) and *The Years Between*

(1919), 58–60; W. G. T. Shedd, *The Complete Works of Samuel Taylor Coleridge* (1853), I.435–6; T. E. Lawrence, *Seven Pillars of Wisdom* (1935), 57; John Milton, *The Fifth Ode of Horace, Lib 1*; David Hume, Letter to the Rev. Hugh Blair, September 19, 1763; G.-H. Gaillard, *Mélanges Académiques, Poétiques, Littéraires, Philologiques, Critiques et Historiques* (1806), II.2; *Proceedings of the Cotteswold Naturalists' Club* 1 (1853), *Appendix* p. 10; John Dryden, *A Discourse Concerning the Original and Progress of Satire* (1693).

Horace

Index

Index

Horace